Contents

Introduction vi

Level one 1

1 **Factual accounts for forms** 2
Run of bad luck

2 **Advice leaflets** 5
'Well now, Mr Johnston . . .'

3 **Descriptions of machines** 9
'I've got this great idea!'

4 **Instructions** 12
A patchy performance

5 **Directions** 15
'Where am I?'

6 **Personal reports** 18
The piper
Grandad with snails
MICHAEL BALDWIN

7 **Eyewitness statements** 22
Towering inferno

Level two 25

8 **Talks intended to persuade** 26
Tobacco: the facts
Drug abuse briefing
MIKE ASHTON

9 **Radio commentaries** 30
The death of a king

10 **Advice in newspapers and magazines** 33
Mugging

11 Formal letters making arrangements **37**
Preparing the way

12 Articles for school magazines **41**
A brave experiment
The Secret Diary of Adrian Mole Aged 13¾
SUE TOWNSEND

13 Personal letters to persuade **44**
Taste for adventure

14 Newspaper articles **48**
A table for two
Mapp and Lucia
E F BENSON

15 Situation reports in letter form **52**
Saltash Bridge
The Building of Saltash Bridge
W HEATH ROBINSON

16 Application letters and *curricula vitae* **54**
Write for the job

Level three **57**

17 Advertising material **58**
Sinclair's electric buggy
Loophole Wagon THE TIMES

18 Debate speeches **62**
Anyone for marriage?

19 Reports making comparisons **64**
Snap decision

20 Formal letters of complaint **68**
The Test
ANGELICA GIBBS

21 Formal letters making suggestions **73**
Warning: children crossing

22 Publicity for causes **77**
The egg factory
The Case for Cages
THE NATIONAL FARMERS' UNION
Song of the Battery Hen
EDWIN BROCK

23 **Letters to The Editor** — **81**
Teenage attitudes

24 **Discussion and minutes of meetings** — **85**
An exchange of views

25 **Articles reporting surveys** — **87**
Teenage lives

Resource File — **91**

Index of language types — **119**

Introduction

We have surely grown accustomed in recent years to the notion that language must be used *appropriately* if it is to be effective. And quite clearly this is true. There is an obvious need to adjust the way we write (and, of course, speak) to the context: to our subject matter, the language form we are using, the 'audience' we are addressing and our purpose in writing.

Yet it is only with the introduction of 16+ English syllabuses that we have been obliged to explore in any depth with our pupils this idea of appropriateness. The traditional summary and composition based on essentially literary forms demand, for example, no marked awareness of a particular reader nor does the writer need to have in mind any objective that lies outside the writing itself.

Now, however, pupils are required to display competence in a wider range of writing tasks, many of them of a more 'practical' nature. In addition to the conventional composition, they are expected to be able to write sets of instructions and directions, eye-witness statements, letters of different kinds, publicity material, reports and so forth. Not only must they be familiar with a greater number of language forms than formerly but also most of the additional tasks they may be called on to perform certainly do require a very strong realisation of context – a clear sense of audience and purpose, in particular.

Despite the increased demands being made on their pupils and provided there is no move to devalue personal, creative writing, teachers will doubtless welcome this recognition of the socially instrumental nature of language and approve of the practical purposiveness of many of the writing tasks pupils are now set.

Graded Practice in Writing for a Purpose is largely concerned with such tasks. Its main intention is to provide varied and lively assignments that will help young writers to develop the versatility and sense of appropriateness they must now display in **final examination papers** and in **coursework folders** – indeed, it is hoped that some of the completed assignments will find a place in these folders.

Each of the twenty-five units is primarily devoted to a particular species of writing which may be defined by reference to the language form used (a letter, a report, a set of instructions, etc), the purpose in writing (to persuade, to convey facts clearly, to sell a product, etc) and the nature of the audience addressed. The unit headings give some indication of these topics, though the specification of audience and purpose is often more conveniently left to the exercise instructions. The scope of the book in terms of the varieties of language covered will be found in the index.

The sources

The material with which units begin and which provides the stimulus for the first exercise comes from a miscellany of sources and itself takes a variety of forms: passages of fiction, drawings, poetry, maps, dialogue, photographs, extracts from brochures and so on. The aim is not simply to offer an interestingly diverse selection but also to encourage pupils to understand and use information presented in very different ways – including statistical information exhibited in various formats. Though some teachers may be rather wary of introducing material of this last type into their lessons, in fact pupils do tend to enjoy scrutinising statistical data and can be remarkably astute in recognising their implications, especially when they relate to matters which directly concern them. The desirability here of class discussion, in groups perhaps, is obvious, but it is suggested that more generally pupils be given opportunities to discuss the initial material: most of the units invite this, both as an activity valuable in itself and as a prerequisite for successful written work later.

The first two exercises

Although exercise 1 is based on this initial material, it usually calls for a more 'creative' response than the mere re-presentation of extracted information: pupils need, for example, to interpret the material, supplement and correct it, develop it imaginatively or formulate an attitude towards it. It is hoped that this more active involvement will serve to enliven the assignments and to avoid the impression some textbooks – and indeed, some public examinations – can give that functional writing is a pedestrian chore.

The second exercise offers a choice of further tasks which require writing of the type introduced in exercise 1 – this time unrelated to the initial material.

There will probably be two main ways in which teachers choose to make use of these exercises. After preparatory discussion, pupils may be set exercise 1 as their individual assignments, in which case exercise 2 could be used at some later date to provide additional practice in the same type of writing should it be felt necessary. Alternatively, teachers may prefer to employ exercise 1 in their exposition of the requirements of the language use under consideration, perhaps working the exercise on the blackboard as a joint effort. Pupils would then be assigned exercise 2 to complete independently. It will be found that some units lend themselves more readily to the first approach and others to the second.

Optional extras

The exercises headed *Other writing*, calling as they do for conventional descriptive, narrative and discursive compositions, might be thought out of place in a book that professes to be concerned with the more functional aspects of language. Certainly they are offered very much as optional extras which teachers might wish to pass over. However, it seemed sensible to suggest the opportunities for such work presented by the material and a useful way of reminding ourselves that no English course can afford to neglect the traditional essay.

Grading in three levels

It was thought that teachers would appreciate some attempt to grade the demands the book makes on their pupils, though this has not proved easy to do. Most of the tasks are accessible to a wide range of ability and are so disparate in the skills they require that trying to develop an order of ascending difficulty yielded very arbitrary results. Nevertheless, the grouping of units on three levels is a compromise which may be found helpful and certainly reflects the author's experience in using the material with his own pupils. The order in which units within each group are presented to a class must, however, be a matter for the teacher's own judgement.

The Resource File

Exercises frequently refer pupils to the Resource File, an important feature of the book which comprises examples of kinds of language with which pupils may not be too familiar as well as items of a more commonplace sort – advertisements, for example – which teachers may wish to examine closely and therefore pupils need to have before them.

Level one

1 Factual accounts for forms

Run of bad luck

Hillcrest Garden Products Ltd
Freemantle Estate
Coventry
CV7 5TH

Telephone: (0203) 10314
Telex: 89251

Our reference: JCG/SM/14
Your reference:

K. Gillham Esq.,
27 Fairfield Road,
Scunthorpe.

26th July, 19-

Dear Sir,

Thank you for your letter of 17th July. Whilst we are naturally most sympathetic concerning the unfortunate events which involved our RM14 Rotary Lawnmower, we cannot agree that Hillcrest are in any way responsible nor can we entertain your claim for compensation.

As you rightly say, our operating manual nowhere advises against adjusting the mower in your living room; however, it does clearly state that the machine must be disconnected from the mains prior to such adjustments. We much regret the damage to your sheepskin hearthrug and coffee-table but cannot accept that we are at fault.

Similarly, the instructions stress the danger from flying objects - stones and so forth - likely to result if the RM14 is operated without its grassbox in place. What occurred when the mower ran over your cigarette-lighter was therefore utterly predictable. Thank goodness the missile struck only your glass-fronted display-cabinet and not someone's head!

Finally, page 17 of the manual does warn against inadvertently moving the machine over its own cable. Obviously your mind was on other things at the time, but we cannot answer for the electric shock which threw you into the hi-fi system and led to the unpleasantness with the cat.

We hope you appreciate our position in this matter. Perhaps your best course would be to contact your insurance firm in the normal way.

Yours faithfully,

John C. Glover

General Manager

Writing for a purpose

1 Taking the advice given at the end of the letter, Mr Gillham makes an insurance claim for the damage to his property. He is required to complete this form:

STAR ASSURANCE LTD

Home Contents Claim Form

Name of Insured ______________________ Policy No. ______________

Address ______________________ Telephone No. ______________

1 What was the date and time of the occurrence? ______________

2 What property was lost/damaged? (Please submit estimates for repair/replacement with this form.) ______________

____

____

3 How did the loss/damage occur? (Please state the circumstances fully.) ______________

____

____

Copy out the form and then, using your imagination to reconstruct the incident from the evidence given in the letter, fill it in as Mr Gillham might have done. What is needed in answer to question 3 is a detailed factual account of how each item listed under 2 came to be damaged. (See Resource 1, page 92.)

2 Imagine an occurrence which leads you to do one of the following, all of which would involve you in form-filling:

a make an accident report of the sort that education authorities require when a mishap at school results in injury;

b submit an insurance claim after a road accident or a small fire in your home;

c complain to the Race Relations Board or the Equal Opportunities Commission about an instance of racial or sexual discrimination.

Write a detailed account of the occurrence as it would appear on the form. A very factual piece of writing concerning an event which requires several sentences to describe fully is what is called for here. (See Resource 1, page 92.)

Other writing

A Question of Luck
Write one of the following:

a a short story on the theme of luck – an account perhaps of how a stroke of good or bad luck completely changed someone's life, or of a day when everything that could go wrong did;

b an essay in which you discuss the subject of luck from any point of view that interests you; you could, for example, consider the extent to which a successful, happy life depends on good luck, or examine the superstitious beliefs many of us have about good and bad luck, or discuss the view that we are born either lucky or unlucky and there is little we can do to change the situation.

2 Advice leaflets

'Well now, Mr Johnston . . .'

The local branch of Associated Insurance Services has a staff vacancy. The Manageress is sufficiently impressed by Robert's letter of application to want to see him. Now everything depends on how successfully he can handle the interview.

1 The start

(*Mrs Milne is working at her desk. Her secretary enters and shows a young man into the office.*)

SECRETARY Mr Robert Johnston is here, Mrs Milne.

MRS MILNE Ah, Mr Johnston. We'd almost given you up. Trouble with the buses?

ROBERT No. I overslept.

MRS MILNE I see. No, don't sit there. You'll find this chair more comfortable. Would you like a cup of tea?

ROBERT I wouldn't say no.

MRS MILNE Two teas then please, Miss Hollins.
(*The secretary leaves.*)
Well now, I've got your letter here and . . . Is there something wrong?

ROBERT Have you got an ashtray?

MRS MILNE To your left there. So then, you say you'll be taking six GCSEs and you list them here. How do you think you'll do?

ROBERT It's difficult to say, isn't it?

MRS MILNE Do you think you'll pass them all?

ROBERT I'm not sure about French. I should get the rest though. Of course, I couldn't say what grades.

MRS MILNE Which do you feel is your best subject?

ROBERT Maths. I'm not bad at Maths.

MRS MILNE You enjoy that, do you?

ROBERT It's all right.

MRS MILNE You don't sound very keen.

ROBERT No, it's all right . . .

2 The middle

ROBERT . . . But then I blame this Conservative Government.

MRS MILNE Right, let's move on. Let's look at your interests. Are you involved in any school activities – outside the classroom I mean?

ROBERT I do some sport.

MRS MILNE Which?

ROBERT Oh, football and a bit of athletics.

MRS MILNE Are you much good?

ROBERT Well, I'm in the school football team – the first eleven.

MRS MILNE Any other school interests?

ROBERT Not really. I suppose there's the History Society. I go along to all their meetings.

MRS MILNE You're interested in History then, are you?

ROBERT It's all right.

MRS MILNE What about responsibilities in school? Do you have any?

ROBERT Not really.

MRS MILNE But in his reference your headmaster says you're a house games captain.

ROBERT Oh, if you count that, yes. But it's just drawing up team lists and things.

MRS MILNE How do you spend your time outside school? Do you do anything interesting?

ROBERT I watch a bit of telly, go out with my mates – that sort of thing.

MRS MILNE What do you do with your friends?

ROBERT Oh you know, just generally messing around: the amusement arcade, the odd party – that sort of thing.

MRS MILNE The reference from Mr Simpson . . . Who's he, by the way?

ROBERT He runs the youth club.

MRS MILNE You belong to a youth club?

ROBERT Yes.

MRS MILNE He says you spend a lot of time raising money for the National Children's Home.

ROBERT Oh yes, there's that. Most weekends I'm involved one way or another.

MRS MILNE Well go on, tell me about that . . .

3 The end

MRS MILNE . . . You'd enjoy working in insurance, would you?

ROBERT Well, let's face it: you've got to take whatever you can get these days, haven't you? The damned employment situation being what it is.

MRS MILNE Is there any special reason you applied to us rather than some other insurance firm?

ROBERT Yours was the only advert I saw.

MRS MILNE Do you know anything about us? What sort of insurance we specialise in, for example?

ROBERT I can't say I do.

MRS MILNE If we took you on, we'd expect you to continue studying. In your case that would mean the Business Education Council national certificate first. There's half-day release to allow you to do that. So how would you feel about it – carrying on with your studies I mean?

ROBERT Sounds fair enough.

MRS MILNE It would mean working at home, of course.

ROBERT I suppose so.

MRS MILNE Well now, is there anything you'd like to ask me?

ROBERT What's the pay?

MRS MILNE I've got some salary information here; you can take the sheet away with you. Is there anything else?

ROBERT I don't think so.

MRS MILNE In that case, Mr Johnston, I think we've covered everything. Thank you for coming. We'll be writing to you in a day or two.

ROBERT That's it then, is it?

MRS MILNE Yes, thank you. Goodbye.

(*Robert gets up and leaves the office. Mrs Milne sighs deeply.*)

Writing for a purpose

1 Robert was not offered the job – hardly surprising in view of the poor impression he made at the interview. Discuss the ways you consider he failed to do himself justice and the general lessons that can be learned about how best to prepare oneself for interviews and to conduct oneself at them. Then produce a leaflet which summarises these lessons and could be given to young people in their final year at school. Your advice should be very straightforward and clearly set out and worded. (See Resource 2, pages 93 and 94.)

2 Write a leaflet giving basic advice to someone who:
a is planning to buy a pet for the first time;

- **b** intends to try a walking, cycling or camping holiday;
- **c** wants to become and stay fit;
- **d** is thinking of organising a disco, a sponsored event or a children's party;
- **e** is about to enter the first year at your school; or
- **f** wants to take up a particular sport.

(See Resource 2, pages 93 and 94.)

Other writing

On the Carpet
Being subjected to close questioning, whoever is doing the probing – an employer, the police, a headteacher, parents or a friend – can be a nerve-racking experience, producing a mixture of feelings and strong reactions. Show this to be true in a short story – true or imagined – in which you find yourself undergoing interrogation of some kind.

3 Descriptions of machines

'I've got this great idea!'

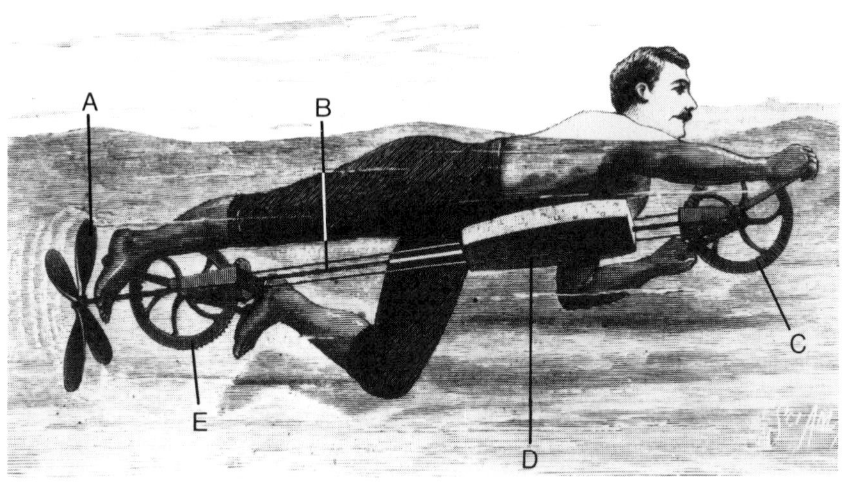

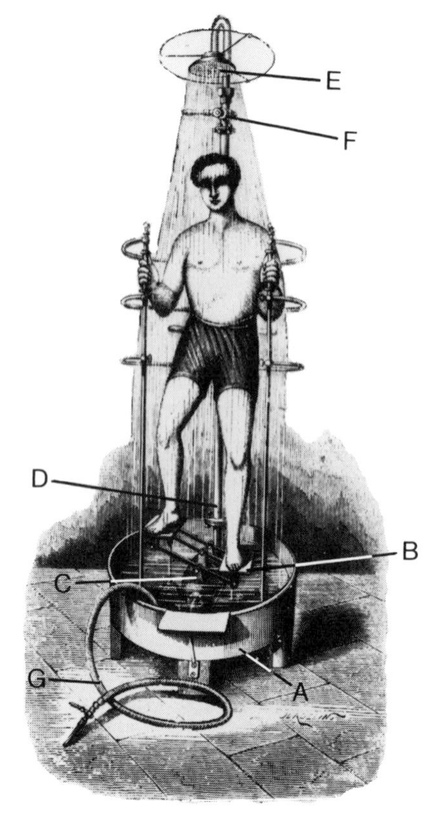
E
F
D
B
C
G
A

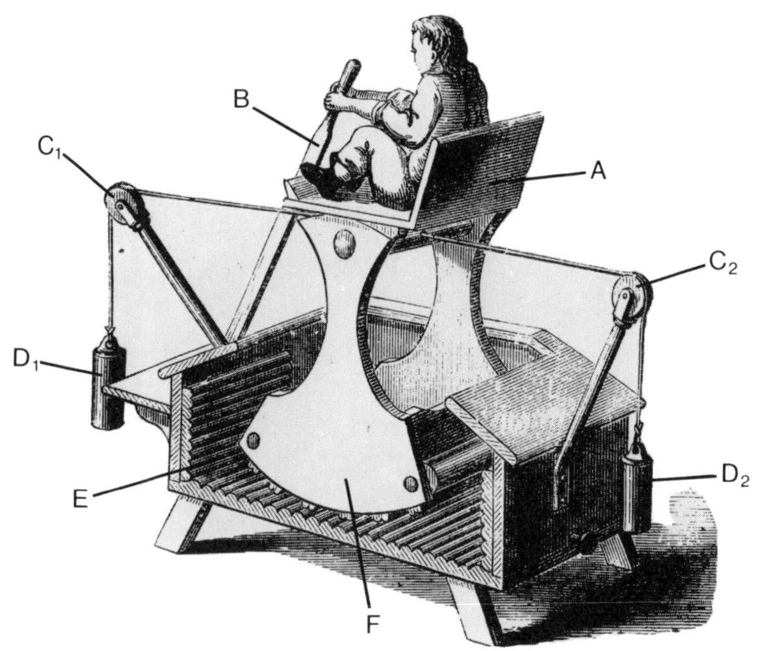
B
C_1
A
C_2
D_1
D_2
E
F

Writing for a purpose

1 It is usual for inventors to protect their ideas by registering them with the Government Patent Office. They do this by submitting a drawing, together with a very clear explanation of what the invention is designed to do, how it is constructed and the way it is meant to work.

Produce such explanations for any two of the devices illustrated on pages 9 or 10. It is not obvious in every case what purpose the inventor had in mind – you will have to decide for yourself. Parts of the machines have been lettered to make it easier for you to refer to them if you need to do so. (See Resource 3, page 95.)

2 Design a piece of equipment to perform some supposedly useful task; for example, a burglar alarm that also stops the intruder escaping, a machine that not only wakes you up but makes sure you get out of bed, an automatic egg-boiler and bread-toaster that will have your breakfast waiting for you in the morning, a snooper-deterrer that gives anyone prying in your room a surprise he or she will never forget.

Try to avoid making use of already existing devices like electric motors or clocks. The odder your invention, the better, but at least in theory it should work.

You should then prepare a neat drawing of your brain-child, labelled if you wish, and a clear description of its purpose, its construction and how it operates. (See Resource 3, page 95.)

Other writing

Back to the Drawing-board

We can imagine that when machines like those opposite and on page 9 are actually tried out, things do not always go to plan. Write an account of such a test which has results that are embarrassing, disastrous, hilarious or all three.

4 Instructions

A patchy performance

You do not have to be a genius to mend a puncture – however:

DAVID You're sure there are no instructions in the repair-kit?

KIRSTY Look for yourself if you don't believe me. Hadn't we better wait till dad gets home?

DAVID Oh come on, Kirsty; all it needs is a bit of common sense. Anyway, we've got your wheel off now so we might just as well press on.

KIRSTY All right then, let's get the inner-tube out. Pass me the tyre-levers. It's just a matter of prising the side of the tyre over the rim of the wheel – like this.

DAVID Go easy with those levers or you'll tear the inner-tube.

KIRSTY There, that's one side of the tyre off. Should I take it off completely?

DAVID No need: you ought to be able to get the inner-tube out now. First push the valve up out of the wheel.

KIRSTY I can't. It's stuck.

DAVID There's a locknut holding the valve in place, moron. Unscrew it. Hey presto, one extracted inner-tube! Now I'll just pump it up.

KIRSTY Should I get a bowl of water? You put the inner-tube in water and look for bubbles, don't you?

DAVID Hang on; let's see if we can hear it hissing first. Yes, look: there's the hole.

KIRSTY Keep your eye on it. There's a little pencil in the repair-kit. Here you are; mark where the hole is.

DAVID So far so good. Told you there was nothing to it.

KIRSTY David, what's this grater-thing for?

DAVID Grater-thing?

KIRSTY Yes, look – like you grate cheese with but smaller. Then there's this bit of sandpaper and a block of something – chalk or something. What're they for?

DAVID Were they in the kit?

KIRSTY Yes. What're they meant for?

DAVID Search me.

KIRSTY But they've got to be for something, haven't they?

DAVID Kirsty.

KIRSTY Yes, David?

DAVID Stop asking idiot questions and keep your mind on the job. Right, now I'll let the air out of the tube; it'll make it easier to press the patch down firmly. Have you got one ready?

KIRSTY Is this big enough?

DAVID Looks all right. Which side goes next to the tube – the rubbery orange side or the plasticky white side?

KIRSTY David.

DAVID Yes, Kirsty?

KIRSTY Stop asking idiot questions. The white side's just backing; it peels off.

DAVID So it does. You amaze me sometimes, Kirsty. Okay, squeeze some glue round the hole.

KIRSTY How much?

DAVID Not much. Just enough to cover the area of the patch.

KIRSTY Should I put some on the patch too?

DAVID Might as well. Right now, let me stick the patch on while the glue's still runny; this stuff dries fast.

KIRSTY Press it down hard.

DAVID Great! Now what? Should we get the tube back in?

KIRSTY Better wait a bit and let it dry. Then all we've got to do is put everything together again.

DAVID It's dead easy, this puncture business, isn't it? Told you we wouldn't need instructions.

Writing for a purpose

1 Although David is obviously very pleased with himself at the end of the dialogue, instructions would certainly have helped them avoid a number of mistakes. Discuss their attempt and try to decide where they went wrong; then compile a set of numbered instructions that could be included in a puncture-repair outfit.

Such kits are used by a great variety of people, some of them very young and inexperienced in this sort of job, so your instructions will need to be detailed and worded simply and clearly. Unit 2 in this book involved the writing of advice leaflets; what you are required to do in this exercise is rather similar, but, of course, advice and instruction are different things and you should consider how this difference will affect the way you organise your material and indeed the tone of your writing. (See Resource 4, page 96.)

2 Write a clear set of numbered instructions which would enable

someone who had never done so before to perform some complicated task with which you are familiar. You could choose – though you do not have to – one of the following:
putting up a tent; house-training a dog; changing a baby's nappy; replacing a broken window-pane; washing and styling someone's hair; making jam; administering first aid to someone with a fracture.
You may provide a diagram if you feel it would help. (See Resource 4, page 96.)

Other writing

Sounds Natural
As an exercise in writing dialogue that captures the way people really speak, invent a few minutes of one of these conversations:

a a family try to agree on what holiday, if any, they should take next summer or on who should do which jobs around the house;
b two or three friends discuss a particularly interesting piece of local scandal;
c you work your way round to making an unwelcome announcement to your parents or the people with whom you live; for example, that you have got engaged, been suspended from school, invited half a dozen friends to stay for the weekend, had yourself tattooed or invested your building society money in a drum-kit.

You will realise, of course, that the English we speak differs from the English we write; you should certainly not suppose, however, that your dialogue will be realistic simply because you have packed it with slang (or worse), dropped every 'h' and been hopelessly ungrammatical.

5 Directions

'Where am I?'

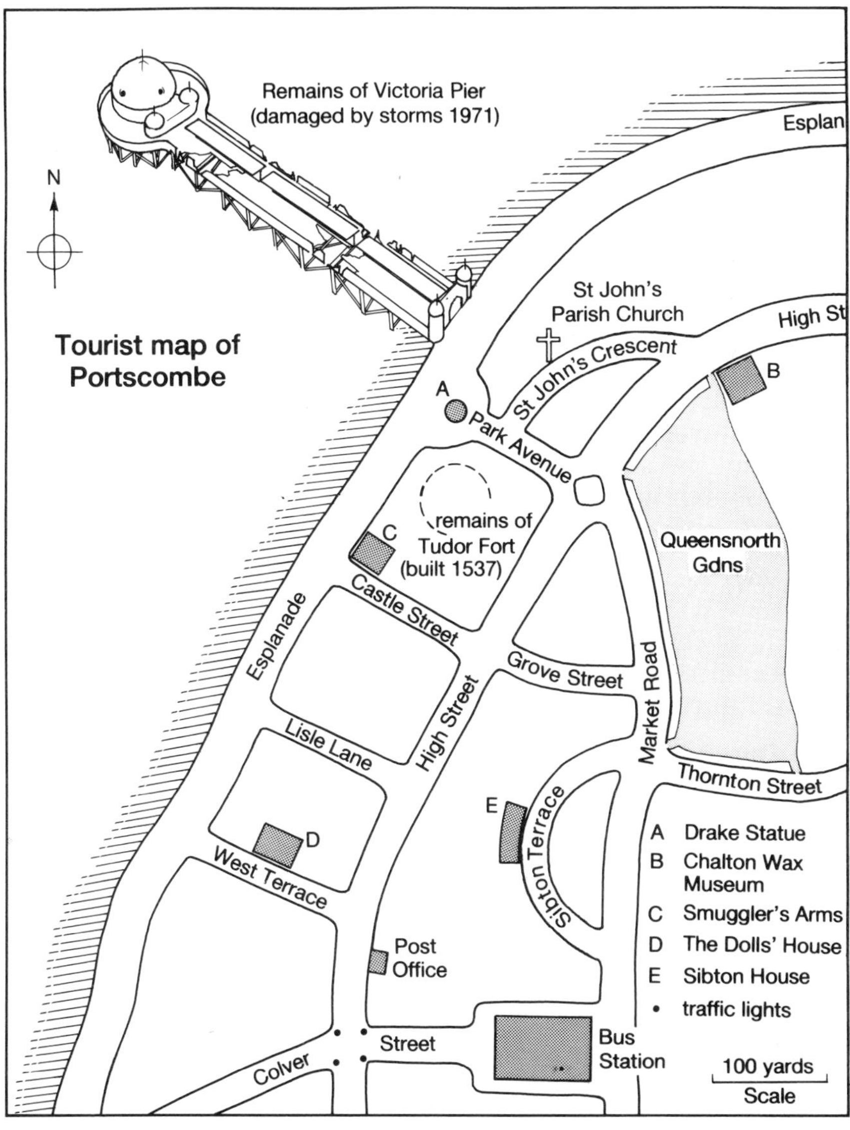

Extracts from the Official Guide to Portscombe

The Smuggler's Arms A 400-year-old, thatched coaching inn which retains much of its old-world character, with low-beamed ceilings, log fires in winter, local prints and, it is said, an original sixteenth-century ghost. Walled garden with skittle alley. Children's room and small restaurant.

St John's Parish Church Partly Norman but largely rebuilt in the eighteenth century. Of special note are the tomb slabs in the chancel aisle and the early stained glass of the circular window behind the altar. Some of the gravestones in the churchyard bear interesting inscriptions.

Chalton Wax Museum (Admission 85p, children 60p. Open 10 am–7 pm daily May to Sept.) The handsome half-timbered building houses tableaux depicting scenes from local and national history in startling realism. The Chamber of Horrors contains a gruesome collection of instruments of torture, and Portscombe's less respectable past is recreated in the Smuggler's Den. Fine period furniture and costumes. Recorded commentaries. Refreshments, toilets and nearby parking.

Queensnorth Gardens (Admission free. Open throughout the year.) These delightful gardens, established in the early 1920s, offer a peaceful haven close to the town centre. Quiet tree-lined walks wind between richly stocked flower-beds, shrubberies, lawns and rockeries, and the visitor will be charmed by the sunken rose-garden and the lily ponds. Floodlit during summer evenings.

The Dolls' House (Admission 50p. Open throughout the year, 9.30 am–6 pm.) Lovingly assembled over forty years by proprietress Miss Sybil Crawley, the exhibition comprises some 300 toys and dolls, many of them Victorian and wearing their original clothes. The pride of the collection is a rag doll once owned by the present queen.

The Francis Drake Statue Presented to the town in 1931 by a former mayor, Elizabeth Etherby, this imposing bronze figure gazing towards the French coast commemorates the famous explorer's association with Portscombe in which he lived for six years. The work of the celebrated sculptor Sir Alfred Graves RA.

Sibton House (Admission 70p, children 40p. Open Tuesday & Fridays, May to Oct., 2–6 pm.) One of an elegant terrace of Regency dwellings, the home of Edward Scott, Victorian dramatist and poet, during his last years. The house is furnished much as Scott left it, and it was in the oak-panelled study that he penned his well known 'Portscombe Down'. A fascinating collection of original manuscripts.

Writing for a purpose

1 The town's Tourist Information Centre publishes a booklet called *Short Walks in and around Portscombe*. The walks in the town itself all begin and end at the Bus Station, and, of course, are carefully planned to include as many places of interest as possible. There is a map of each walk but since people often seem to find these difficult to understand, precise directions are also provided.

Plan such a tourist walk through the area of Portscombe shown on the map and then prepare the written description of the route. Your directions must be easy to follow and you should say a little about whatever is of interest on the tour, including attractions the visitor might be encouraged to pay to enter. You will find the excerpts from the official guide useful, though they contain more detail than you require. (See Resource 5, page 97.)

2 Imagine that either your school or some particularly drab part of your locality is in fact a tourist attraction which draws many visitors. Plan a sight-seeing tour through whichever you have chosen and write a set of very clear directions, pointing out supposed places of interest that will be met along the way. You will find that the more apparently serious and enthusiastic you are about what you are describing, the more amusing the result will be. (See Resource 5, page 97.)

Other writing

The Spirit of the Place
Like people, places have their own individual character – sometimes attractive, sometimes unpleasant, often dull – and it is this character and individuality that a thoughtful piece of description will try to capture. Bearing this in mind, write a description, in the form of a poem if you wish, of somewhere you know well: an area of a town or city, a village, a stretch of countryside or even a single building, your home perhaps. Select your details and the words in which you describe them carefully to convey the 'feel' of the place.

Lost!
Most of us have recollections of finding ourselves completely lost. For a child separated from its parents in some unfamiliar place, for example, it can be a terrifying ordeal, but even when we are older, having absolutely no idea where we are can be very alarming. Write a story – preferably a true one – with this theme, trying to convey the feelings involved.

6 Personal reports

The piper

Then the door opened.

Two of the girls saw, and whispered excitedly. Miss Rose just went pale.

Into the room, after a long pause, stepped a pair of legs ragged up to the knees, and bare, shockingly so, in places above the knees. So nearly naked were the legs that it was some time before I looked up past an unravelling pullover and saw a rather pallid fourteen-year-old face, completely without teeth, fidgeting brown eyes, and layers of dirty curly hair. The toothless mouth grinned. ''Lo, Miss Rose,' it said; speaking made the face look like a torn bag of soot.

'It's Poiper,' said somebody.

'Piper! – his dad's back 'ome, then. Went off with a gipsy woman.'

''Allo, Bill. 'Allo, Tom,' he said, in the pause that followed. ''Ow's the snares going? Did you have any luck? I knew you would.'

Miss Rose moved towards him and was speaking at last.

'Alan Piper!'

''Allo, Miss Rose. 'Ow's yer 'usband? O no, Ma said 'ee wouldn't marry you.'

We roared our appreciation.

'Alan Piper – have you come back to school?'

'Yes, miss. Dad's back.'

'A pity he can't find some decent garments for your back!'

'These are Dad's duds. What more can he do? Don't you go on about Dad. 'Ee's all right.'

'Well, if you're here you'd better sit down. No, not there with the girls. Go to the back where no one can see you.'

'If you say so. I'm nothing to be ashamed of.' As he walked past we noticed he smelled a little, nothing much.

'Have you brought any lunch?'

'No-o. I got friends. All right, Tom? Share your sandwich?'

Tom nodded. The lesson settled down.

'We're doing sums,' said Miss Rose.

He perked up a little at that.

'Sums,' he said. 'What use is sums?' He had thought about this problem. Miss Rose hadn't. 'Dad says sums is a lot of fuss about things you can do better in your 'ead; 'ee says it's like counting animals' legs and dividing by four; 'ee says you always find you've counted in their tails anyway; 'ee says . . .'

Miss Rose hit him.

'Oo,' he said. 'Oo dear me!'

Miss Rose pretended she had won and walked back to the blackboard. 'You ignorant baby,' she said. 'You ought to be ashamed.'

'I am, miss.'

He put his hand up after a while. Miss Rose was surprised by this show of politeness. 'Yes, Alan Piper?' she asked.

'Miss, if you was to see a blue egg, about as long as your thumbnail, with pinky spots on it like your chin, what bird would it be?'

'I'm sure I don't know,' she answered, keeping calm with difficulty.

'Never you mind, miss. I'll ask you another. Suppose you was poaching rabbit, and suppose . . .'

'Oh stop wasting my time, Piper!'

'Miss . . . when do teachers ever learn anything useful? Why should you pretend to know more than me? You've not even got a baby – I have, miss. Don't you know that?'

Miss Rose looked at the clock. 'Dinner,' she said.

''Fore you move,' said Piper, 'I'll collect me sandwiches. All true sports'll give one each.'

We were all true sports.

After school that evening – we'd done no work since his arrival – he marched round to the front of the Village Hall where about ten girls were waiting for him. 'Be careful of that bike,' he said. 'I've only just stole it,' he added, as we stood shy in the background, and the girls tittered.

'See the gents in the morning,' he called, and he went off laughing with the girls, his bare legs brown in the sun. When the village policeman came round the corner they surrounded the Piper and he walked happily on.

A few days later Mr Noake, the headmaster, sat in on Miss Rose's lesson.

The lesson began and the Piper even put his hand up twice. Once was when Miss Rose asked who had discovered the North West Passage and Piper answered eagerly, 'The Vicar.' Noake picked up his cane and replaced it on the desk. The second time was to do with gunpowder. Miss Rose had already told us a minute before that it was invented by the Chinese, and Noake looked up sharply at this and interrupted her, trying to catch him, '*Who* invented gunpowder, Piper?'

'My father,' answered Piper with conviction.

Noake leapt up with a snarl and brought down his cane. 'It was a Chinaman,' he roared.

'My father's a Chinaman,' muttered the Piper.

'So, *Mr* Piper. I'm getting a little bit tired of you,' hissed Noake. 'The school cannot tolerate this sort of behaviour.'

'Dad left yesterday,' said the Piper. 'And if Dad's left, I don't see 'ows I'm to stay.'

'*Bend over*,' roared Noake.

'No,' said the Piper, with dignity. 'I'm not dressed for it.'

'Very well, then.' And Noake was upon him, lashing at him with his cane, pushing him, beating him down. We had never seen him launch such an attack.

The Piper ran round him in a circle held by Noake's great left hand, and the thin cane rose and fell, and the Piper's voice seemed to be cut into the air.

But he did not cry. He swore. And he did not swear aimlessly. He swore at Noake – strange hedge-oaths, gipsy oaths, Bible words. Noake flogged him, as he twisted and writhed and we watched in terror, waiting for him to beat himself to a standstill.

After a long time he stopped, and breathed triumphantly while the Piper stood up.

'Now apologise,' said Noake, still rich in the face.

The Piper looked at him, dead white.

'*Apologise*,' stormed Noake.

The Piper reached out his hand, quietly, as a man does to a friend, almost as if he was going to shake hands. Noake half-responded to this strange gesture. In a flash the Piper had his cane and brandished it aloft.

As Noake jumped forward he slashed him across the face, ducked round him and struck him on the shoulders. Before Noake could recover he had run to the door.

For a moment he paused there, smiling at us all. 'See you, Elsie,' he said. Then he broke the cane across his knee and tossed the ends to Noake. The door slammed and he was gone.

MICHAEL BALDWIN
Grandad with Snails

Writing for a purpose

1 The School Attendance Officer learns of Alan Piper's case. After visiting the school and Alan's home and talking to the boy himself, he makes out his report under these headings among others:

Regularity of school attendance
Family background
Health, personal cleanliness and dress
Academic ability and attitude towards learning
General conduct in and out of school and attitude towards discipline.

Copy down the headings and under each make the comment the officer might have written. You may invent details if you wish but the passage contains enough information for you to write something under every heading – a short remark under some, two or three sentences under others. (See Resource 6, page 98.)

2 Being as truthful as you can, write one of the following:

a the report your present headteacher might write about you to send to the head of a school to which you are transferring. The intention is, of course, to give a clear picture of the sort of person you are and how well you have got on at school;

b the report the Careers Officer might file away after interviewing you and obtaining information from the school. Include a record of such things as your studies and how well you are doing in them, your interests and your plans for the future.

Whichever report you choose, you should decide first which headings it should be written under; for example, three of them might be: *Name, Date of birth* and *Academic ability and achievements*. (See Resource 6, page 98.)

Other writing

Originals

Like Piper, many people refuse to conform to what is generally expected in matters of appearance, behaviour, belief and so forth. They go their own way, caring little that others think them strange or disapprove of them. Describe one or two such individualists whom you know or know of. Aim to produce word-portraits which give a clear, strong impression of the individuality of the people you are describing. You may present your work as a poem if you wish.

Being Yourself

Consider this opinion: 'Our individuality is being constantly threatened by pressures applied to us by school, home, friends and society as a whole. We are always having to dress, behave and think as others want, not as we would really prefer. It is almost impossible to be a genuine individual.' How true do you think this view is? Does it reflect your own experience?

7 Eyewitness statements

Towering inferno

Writing for a purpose

1 The photograph shows a fire in an office block in which more than two hundred people lost their lives. Helicopters tried to rescue those trapped on the roof but were beaten back by the flames and smoke.

Imagine that an official inquiry is to be held into the fire to examine such questions as how it started, whether panic contributed to the loss of life and how well the fire services performed their work. In preparation for the inquiry, the police collect written statements from onlookers, survivors, fire officers and helicopter pilots.

Write the statements that might have been produced by a spectator and by one of those listed above who were directly involved. You are not being asked to write a short story; what is needed is an unemotional, very factual report of what you saw and, in the second statement, what you did. The more exact you are about the details of what occurred, the more useful your reports will be.

2 Imagine one of the following situations is true:

a you find yourself innocently caught up in a fight between two gangs of young people;

b due to a rather complicated misunderstanding, a friend you are with is stopped by the store detective as you are both leaving a supermarket, accused of shop-lifting and treated with unnecessary roughness;

c you witness the trail of destruction caused by a lorry when its brakes fail on a hill;

d you are in a shop or post office when an armed robbery takes place.

The police ask you to provide a written statement of what you saw and, where applicable, what you did during the episode. Before you begin, consider what information the police are likely to find useful; for example, if you have chosen to write about situation d, anything you can say about the appearance of the

robber/s would be important, whereas how you were feeling during the raid would probably be irrelevant.

Other writing

Making It Real

It would be possible to read the reports required in the first two exercises and still be left with no strong impression of what it was really like to live through the events described. Consider what is needed in a piece of writing if it is to bring an experience alive for the reader and then write a description or a short story in which you try to do this for one of the situations in Exercises 1 and 2.

Level two

8 Talks intended to persuade

Tobacco: the facts

Tobacco is the dried leaves of a plant that grows in many parts of the world (it will even grow in England). Most tobacco used in this country comes from the United States and is sold in the form of cigarettes. Cigars are made from stronger, darker tobacco rolled up in tobacco leaves, and this stronger tobacco can also be smoked in a pipe. Snuff is powdered tobacco sniffed up the nose.

The drug effect of tobacco is caused by nicotine, a mild stimulant found naturally only in tobacco leaves, which vaporises into the smoke when tobacco is burnt.

The Law and other controls

Selling tobacco to children under sixteen is prohibited. Apart from this, there are no restrictions on sale, other than that the import duty and other taxes should have been paid. At the moment, taxes account for nearly three-quarters of the price of a typical packet of twenty cigarettes.

Under the Independent Broadcasting Authority Act of 1973, cigarettes are not allowed to be advertised on television, though TV adverts can still feature other tobacco products such as pipe tobacco and cigars.

The tobacco industry has entered into voluntary agreements which regulate tobacco advertising. For instance, advertisements should not associate smoking with masculinity, virility, femininity, sexual success, achievement or courage, and they should not be aimed at young people.

Extent of use

About 40 per cent of people aged 16 or over are smokers. Until retirement age, the percentage of women cigarette smokers is only a few per cent below the figure for men. Nearly 1 in 5 men and 1 in 10 women smoke sufficient (20+ cigarettes a day) to be classed as heavy smokers.

The smoking habit can start early. Nearly 10 per cent of 13-year-olds smoke at least a cigarette a week, rising to over a quarter at age 15. About 30 per cent of older teenagers smoke.

Short-term use

Cigarette smoke consists of droplets of tar, nicotine, carbon monoxide and other gases. Nicotine and other substances are absorbed by the lungs, so how much is absorbed depends on how much smoke is actually inhaled rather than 'puffed'.

Nicotine is a drug with complex effects on brain activity. One or two cigarettes increase pulse-rate and blood pressure, reduce appetite, lower skin temperature and produce symptoms of stimulation and arousal. Smokers can effectively use smoking to lessen stress and anxiety, but also to maintain performance in the face of fatigue or boredom. Whilst regular smokers experience satisfaction on inhaling, first-time users often feel sick and dizzy.

Long-term use

The body soon gets used to nicotine and larger doses of it are needed to have the same effect. But the more one smokes, the more likely one is to suffer from heart disease, blood clots, heart attacks, lung infections, strokes, bronchitis, bad circulation, lung cancer, cancer of the mouth and throat and ulcers. As a result, tobacco contributes to at least 100,000 premature deaths in the UK every year: a quarter of all young male cigarette smokers will die 'before their time' due to tobacco.

Lung cancer is the disease most closely associated with smoking. Risk of permanent damage to the lungs increases with the number of cigarettes smoked a day, the number of years of smoking and the earliness of the age at which one started. However, if no permanent damage has yet occurred, the lungs will clear themselves once smoking has stopped and the ex-smoker can regain normal health and life-expectancy.

Women who smoke beyond the first months of pregnancy tend to give birth to smaller and less mature babies which may give rise to difficulties after the birth. They also run a slightly increased risk of spontaneous abortion and increase the (still very small) risk of losing the baby around the time of birth.

The most striking aspect of cigarette use is how dependent smokers become on tobacco and how widespread the habit is. People who begin to smoke tend to increase their consumption until they smoke regularly. If they stop, they may feel restless, irritable and depressed, wanting another cigarette. More people are regular users of tobacco than of any other drug.

MIKE ASHTON
Drug Abuse Briefing

Writing for a purpose

1 The passage presents basic information about tobacco in a very factual way; it does not appeal to readers not to smoke – though, of course, some of the facts it contains might be used in such an appeal. Prepare a short talk you could deliver to pupils lower down the school with the intention of discouraging them from cigarette-smoking. Before you begin, you should consider these questions:
   a What should be your general approach? You could try 'shock tactics' in an attempt to scare your listeners off cigarettes, but how effective do you think this approach usually is, especially in the long term?
   b Are there facts about smoking not covered in the passage which you could make use of?
   c How should your material be presented if it is to be understood by a young audience and hold their attention?

2 Write one of the following, which should be aimed at an audience a little younger than yourself:
   a A talk intended to discourage your audience from an activity which you consider dangerous or in some other way undesirable and about which you know enough to talk intelligently. You might choose, for example: drug-taking or solvent-abuse, gambling, under-age drinking, the eating of meat, shop-lifting, vandalism.
   b A talk in which you encourage your listeners to join some organisation you support – for example, St John Ambulance, the Scouts or Guides, the Duke of Edinburgh Award Scheme – or you try to get them to take seriously something you consider important, like road safety, a healthy diet and exercise, tolerance towards racial minorities or controlling pollution.

Other writing

Dying for a Smoke
Certainly cigarette-smoking is a widespread and dangerous habit which raises a number of questions: If smoking is obviously harmful,

why do so many people take it up? Fewer men are smoking now but the number of women smokers is not declining – why? Ought smoking to be made illegal, at least in public where others have the unpleasantness and danger inflicted on them? There are laws banning other harmful drugs, so why is the government apparently so reluctant to act against tobacco? Should there be more restrictions on cigarette advertising – in magazines and on hoardings, for example – and ought tobacco firms to be allowed to continue sponsoring sporting events? Write an essay on the topic of cigarette-smoking, presenting in a carefully argued way your views on some or all of these questions and any other aspects of the subject on which you have opinions. (See Resource 18, page 112.)

9 Radio commentaries

The death of a king

Having overthrown Charles I in the Civil War, the King's political enemies tried him as 'a Tyrant, Traitor and Murderer, and a public enemy to the Commonwealth of England.' He was sentenced to death.

At ten o'clock on the icy, overcast morning of 30th January 1649, having said farewell to the two of his children who remained in England, Charles Stuart left St James's Palace and, wearing two shirts so that he should not shiver and be thought afraid, walked briskly across the park. Rogue, the King's spaniel, made to follow his master but was turned back. Two companies of infantry surrounded their royal prisoner, with drums beating and flags flying, and on the short journey he exchanged a few words with the officer in charge, Colonel Tomlinson, concerning the arrangements for his burial.

Arriving at Whitehall, Charles was conducted to a private room and there left to prepare himself for what was to come. He sat with his chaplain, Bishop Juxon, and the faithful Sir Thomas Herbert, and waited calmly for the summons. He drank one glass of red wine and ate a little bread, sometimes talking with Juxon, sometimes thoughtfully silent. The minutes ticked by.

A black scaffold had been built against the outer wall of the nearby Banqueting Hall and was enclosed by a rail wound in black cloth. The block, similarly draped, was very low – less than ten inches from the floor – so that the King could be more easily tied onto it if he struggled to resist the axe; four iron staples had been driven into the scaffold to take the ropes should this need arise. The common hangman, Richard Brandon, was to perform the beheading and he and his assistant stood ready. They were masked as was the custom but also wore wigs and false beards, so anxious were they to conceal their identities from the public.

It was not until two o'clock that the call came. Charles rose immediately and, leaving Herbert, who was too distressed to witness the coming event, he and his chaplain were escorted to the Banqueting Hall and directed through a window onto the scaffold. There the King was met not only by the grim figures of his executioners but also by the supervising officers, Colonels Tomlinson and Hacker, several guards and two or three shorthand writers, ready to record anything that might be said.

Below a great body of spectators stood in near silence and all could plainly see how greatly their King had aged during the months of his captivity, his hair and beard now grey. Ranks of mounted troopers and foot-soldiers kept the crowd well back from the place of execution, fearful of some public attempt to intervene or a direct appeal from the King to his people. Realising that he could hope to be heard only by those on the scaffold, Charles addressed his last speech to this small audience, referring to notes he had made on a piece of paper four inches square.

He protested himself innocent of all the charges brought against him, maintaining that it was only the determination that his subjects should live in freedom under the old laws, not in fear of the power of the sword, that had brought him to this place: 'and therefore I tell you that I am the Martyr of the people.' He forgave his enemies, professed his belief in the doctrines of the Church of England and then set about his final preparations.

Seeing the block was so low that he would be unable to stoop to it with dignity, Charles turned to the executioner and asked if something higher could be found; Brandon replied, 'It can be no higher, Sir.' The King then explained how he would like the business conducted: he would place his neck and hands on the block and pray for a short while; as the sign that he was ready for the axe, he would move his hands aside. Brandon said he understood.

Helped by Juxon, Charles proceeded to arrange his hair in a white satin cap so that it should not interfere with the blade. With the words, 'I go from a corruptible to an incorruptible Crown, where no disturbance can be, no disturbance in the world,' the King removed the insignia of the Order of the Garter, the only jewel he was wearing, and handed it to Bishop Juxon, adding the simple request: 'Remember'.

Next he took off his cloak and doublet, asked the axeman to confirm that the block was steady and would not move with the blow and, after standing a moment, his eyes and hands towards Heaven, he knelt with his neck resting on the block. Brandon bent to check that the King's hair was out of the way and Charles, thinking he was about to strike, uttered his final sentence: 'Stay for the sign'.

Shortly afterwards Charles Stuart stretched out his arms and instantly the axe fell. Brandon had performed his duties well: the head was cleanly severed from the body with one blow. The executioner raised it aloft with the traditional cry: 'Behold the head of a traitor!' A great groan went up from the crowd, 'such a groan,' remarked one onlooker, 'as I never heard before and desire I may never hear again.'

The troops immediately moved to clear the street. The whole sombre ceremony had taken less than fifteen minutes.

Writing for a purpose

1 If there had been radio broadcasting at the time, doubtless the events described in the passage would have been covered 'live'. Imagine you are giving the commentary for such a broadcast, beginning a few minutes before Charles' arrival on the scaffold. Bear in mind that the skill of a commentator lies in his or her ability to select telling details and present them in a striking way to create vivid mental images for the listener, conveying dramatically the atmosphere of the occasion and, perhaps, the feelings of those taking part.

   You may wish to include interviews with onlookers or officials in the broadcast – perhaps one before the appearance of the King and another after he has died; if so, you should set out your work in dialogue form. (See Resource 7, page 99.)

2 Write a radio commentary similar to the one described in the first exercise, choosing some imaginary or actual event which seems to you suitably dramatic; for example, a state occasion like a royal wedding or funeral, a riot, a large open-air pop festival, the demolition of a skyscraper using explosives or the scene of a motorway pile-up or train derailment. (See Resource 7, page 99.)

Other writing

True Grit

Even Charles' enemies would have to admit that he faced his death courageously; but, of course, courage can take many forms, some of them less dramatic and obvious than the example in the passage. Write one of the following:

a an essay in which you discuss the idea of courage and the different ways in which people may show they are courageous;

b a true or imagined short story, the theme of which is the courage of the main character.

10 Advice in newspapers and magazines

Mugging

Robbery is theft which involves the use or threat of force; mugging is one type of robbery. The police define it as 'robbery of personal property following a sudden attack in the open, the attacker and the victim not being previously known to each other.'

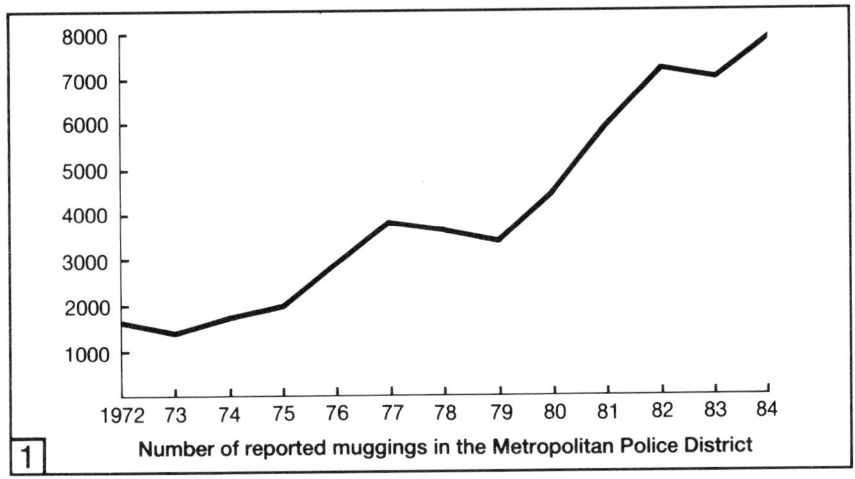

Number of reported muggings in the Metropolitan Police District

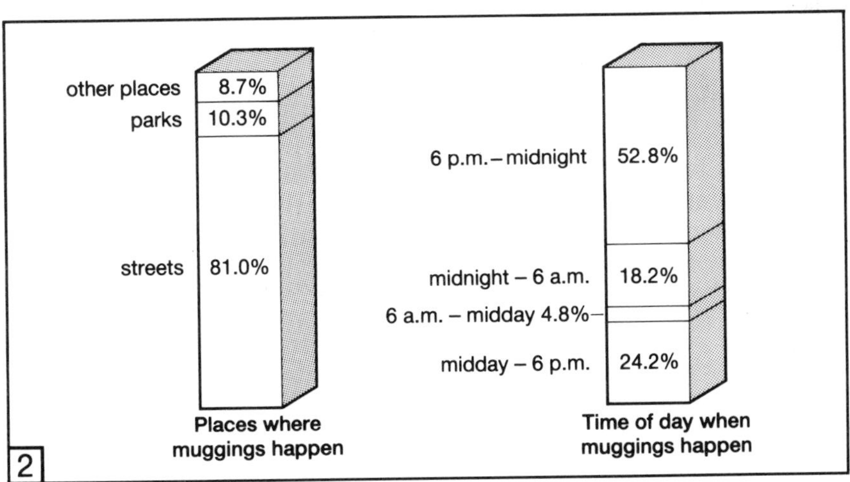

Places where muggings happen

Time of day when muggings happen

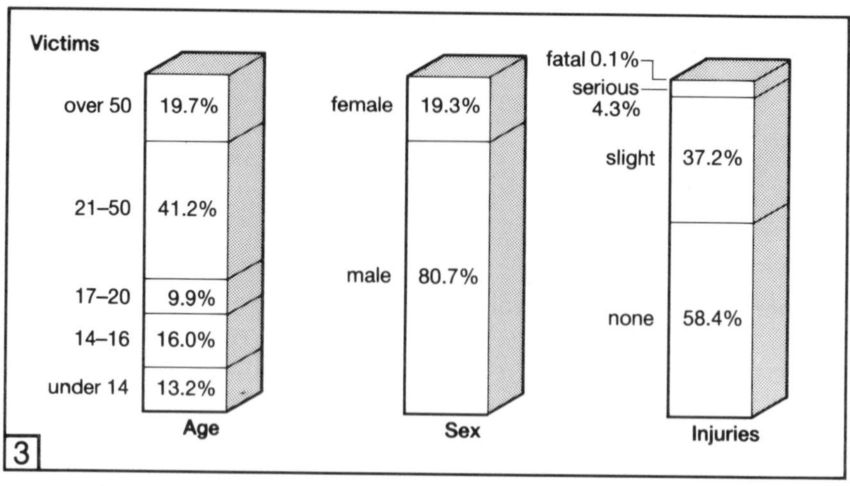

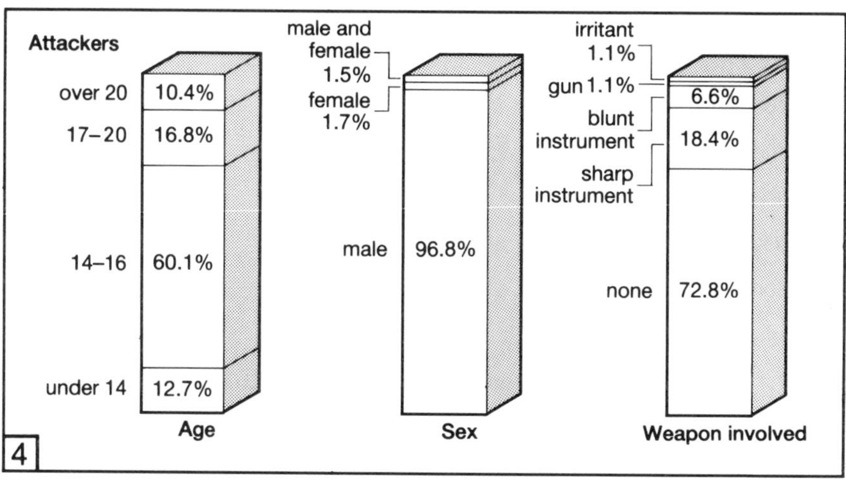

The information in these diagrams concerns the number of reported muggings in recent years, where and when they took place, the sort of people who were attacked and who committed the attacks and the weapons, if any, which were used. These facts relate only to offences committed in the London Metropolitan Police District, not in the country as a whole.

Writing for a purpose

1 This letter appears on the 'problems page' of a newspaper or magazine:

> I am a seventy-two-year-old widow and, like many senior citizens, especially women, who realise they are at special risk from mugging, I live in dread of being attacked when I leave my flat. I used to enjoy spending mornings in the local park but now I never go there or go out at all for that matter unless I have to. What chance would I have against a gang of armed youths or, at my age, of recovering from the terrible injuries muggers usually inflict on their victims? I must say I often feel like a prisoner shut up in my flat.
>
> J Langley
> London

Obviously, what Mrs Langley needs more than anything else is reassurance, and if you study the statistics above, you will see that the situation is not nearly as bad as she believes.

Write a reply that could be printed after this letter. You should use relevant facts revealed by the statistics in an attempt to put Mrs Langley's mind at rest but present them in a way that suggests you are discussing her particular problem sympathetically and at a personal level, not delivering a factual lecture on mugging packed with percentages. (See Resource 8, page 101.)

2 Imagine that these letters are sent to the 'problems page' of a newspaper or magazine and that you have the job of choosing two and offering whatever advice you think would be helpful to the senders. Make sure the reader understands why you are advising him or her the way you are and adopt a suitably sympathetic, personal approach to the problems.

> My fourteen-year-old daughter is always complaining about the strict eye I keep on her social life. She thinks I am most unreasonable when I want to know where she is going in the evenings and with whom, insist she is back by ten o'clock, make her stay in during schoolday evenings and so on. *Am* I being unreasonable in wanting to be a responsible parent?
>
> Mrs Joan Hulton
> Glossop

Our son is adopted, though he does not know it. He is now fifteen and we just cannot decide whether we should tell him we are not his natural parents. We fear it could upset him terribly and spoil our relationship, which at present is very close. What do you suggest?

Mrs R S
Cardiff

My problem is that I'm awfully shy. It may sound stupid but I am terrified of meeting new people and even with classmates I'm dreadfully self-conscious. When I force myself to join in conversations whatever I say sounds feeble and falls flat. Because of all this I hardly ever go out with friends. I usually make excuses when I'm invited to parties etc. I feel very lonely and miserable. What can I do?

Miss M K (16)
Ipswich

Although in other ways my son and I get on extremely well, we find it difficult to discuss very personal matters and we have never talked about the 'facts of life' or personal relationships. He is fifteen now and I tell myself he will already have learned what he needs to know from his school Biology lessons and from friends, so there would be little left for me to do anyway. Am I right, do you think?

Mr E R
Luton

(See Resource 8, page 101.)

Other writing

Going to the Dogs?
It seems to be generally considered that Britain is becoming a very violent, lawless society in which one can no longer feel really safe. What are your own thoughts on the question? Is it your impression that the British are turning increasingly to violence? Support your view with evidence, and if you share the general opinion, suggest reasons why people's behaviour is changing in this way. If you think the country is not such a violent place, can you explain why so many people believe otherwise?

11 Formal letters making arrangements

Preparing the way

SEALINK BRITISH FERRIES — France DOVER – CALAIS

E Dover Eastern Docks – Calais — Crossing about 1hr 30 — Check-in 30 min.
W Dover Western Docks – Calais — Crossing about 1hr 30 — Check-in 30 min.

Latest Information Service
Tel. Dover (0304) 210755

DOVER → CALAIS

AUG			F	S	**S**	M	T	W	T	F	S	**S**	M	T	W	T	F	S	**S**	M	T	W	T	F	S	**S**	M	T	W	T	F	S	**S**
Time			1	2	3	4	5	6	7	8	9	10	11	12	13	14	15	16	17	18	19	20	21	22	23	24	25	26	27	28	29	30	31
0030	**E**	■	D	D	D	D	D	D	D	D	D	D	D	D	D	D	D	D	D	D	D	D	D	D	D	D	D	D	D	D	D	D	D
0130	**E**	▲	D	D	D	D	D	D	D	D	D	D	D	D	D	D	D	D	D	D	D	D	D	D	D	D	D	D	D	D	D	D	D
0300	**E**	▲	D	D	D	D	D	D	D	D	D	D	D	D	D	D	D	D	D	D	D	D	D	D	D	D	D	D	D	D	D	D	D
0500	**E**	■	D	D	D	D	D	D	D	D	D	D	D	D	D	D	D	D	D	D	D	D	D	D	D	D	D	D	D	D	D	D	D
0630	**E**	▲	C	C	C	C	C	C	C	C	C	C	C	C	C	C	C	C	C	C	C	C	C	C	C	C	C	C	C	C	C	C	C
0800	**E**	■	C	C	C	C	C	C	C	C	C	C	C	C	C	C	C	C	C	C	C	C	C	C	C	C	C	C	C	C	C	C	C
0945	**E**	▲	C	C	C	C	C	C	C	C	C	C	C	C	C	C	C	C	C	C	C	C	C	C	C	C	C	C	C	C	C	C	C
1100	**E**	■	C	C	C	C	C	C	C	C	C	C	C	C	C	C	C	C	C	C	C	C	C	C	C	C	C	C	C	C	C	C	C
1300	**E**	■	B	B	B	B	B	B	B	B	B	B	B	B	B	B	B	B	B	B	B	B	B	B	B	B	B	B	B	B	B	B	B
1515	**E**	▲	B	B	B	B	B	B	B	B	B	B	B	B	B	B	B	B	B	B	B	B	B	B	B	B	B	B	B	B	B	B	B
1630	**W**	▲	B	B	B	B	B	B	B	B	B	B	B	B	B	B	B	B	B	B	B	B	B	B	B	B	B	B	B	B	B	B	B
1700	**E**	■	B	B	B	B	B	B	B	B	B	B	B	B	B	B	B	B	B	B	B	B	B	B	B	B	B	B	B	B	B	B	B
1900	**E**	■	B	B	B	B	B	B	B	B	B	B	B	B	B	B	B	B	B	B	B	B	B	B	B	B	B	B	B	B	B	B	B
2030	**E**	▲	C	C	C	C	C	C	C	C	C	C	C	C	C	C	C	C	C	C	C	C	C	C	C	C	C	C	C	C	C	C	C
2145	**E**	▲	C	C	C	C	C	C	C	C	C	C	C	C	C	C	C	C	C	C	C	C	C	C	C	C	C	C	C	C	C	C	C
2300	**E**	■	C	C	C	C	C	C	C	C	C	C	C	C	C	C	C	C	C	C	C	C	C	C	C	C	C	C	C	C	C	C	C

CALAIS → DOVER

AUG			F	S	**S**	M	T	W	T	F	S	**S**	M	T	W	T	F	S	**S**	M	T	W	T	F	S	**S**	M	T	W	T	F	S	**S**
Time			1	2	3	4	5	6	7	8	9	10	11	12	13	14	15	16	17	18	19	20	21	22	23	24	25	26	27	28	29	30	31
0001	**E**	▲	D	D	D	D	D	D	D	D	D	D	D	D	D	D	D	D	D	D	D	D	D	D	D	D	D	D	D	D	D	D	D
0130	**E**	▲	D	D	D	D	D	D	D	D	D	D	D	D	D	D	D	D	D	D	D	D	D	D	D	D	D	D	D	D	D	D	D
0245	**E**	■	D	D	D	D	D	D	D	D	D	D	D	D	D	D	D	D	D	D	D	D	D	D	D	D	D	D	D	D	D	D	D
0500	**E**	▲	D	D	D	D	D	D	D	D	D	D	D	D	D	D	D	D	D	D	D	D	D	D	D	D	D	D	D	D	D	D	D
0630	**E**	■	C	C	C	C	C	C	C	C	C	C	C	C	C	C	C	C	C	C	C	C	C	C	C	C	C	C	C	C	C	C	C
0815	**E**	▲	C	C	C	C	C	C	C	C	C	C	C	C	C	C	C	C	C	C	C	C	C	C	C	C	C	C	C	C	C	C	C
0945	**E**	■	C	C	C	C	C	C	C	C	C	C	C	C	C	C	C	C	C	C	C	C	C	C	C	C	C	C	C	C	C	C	C
1115	**W**	▲	C	C	C	C	C	C	C	C	C	C	C	C	C	C	C	C	C	C	C	C	C	C	C	C	C	C	C	C	C	C	C
1145	**E**	■	C	C	C	C	C	C	C	C	C	C	C	C	C	C	C	C	C	C	C	C	C	C	C	C	C	C	C	C	C	C	C
1315	**E**	▲	B	B	B	B	B	B	B	B	B	B	B	B	B	B	B	B	B	B	B	B	B	B	B	B	B	B	B	B	B	B	B
1500	**E**	■	B	B	B	B	B	B	B	B	B	B	B	B	B	B	B	B	B	B	B	B	B	B	B	B	B	B	B	B	B	B	B
1700	**E**	■	B	B	B	B	B	B	B	B	B	B	B	B	B	B	B	B	B	B	B	B	B	B	B	B	B	B	B	B	B	B	B
1845	**E**	▲	B	B	B	B	B	B	B	B	B	B	B	B	B	B	B	B	B	B	B	B	B	B	B	B	B	B	B	B	B	B	B
2015	**E**	▲	C	C	C	C	C	C	C	C	C	C	C	C	C	C	C	C	C	C	C	C	C	C	C	C	C	C	C	C	C	C	C
2130	**E**	■	C	C	C	C	C	C	C	C	C	C	C	C	C	C	C	C	C	C	C	C	C	C	C	C	C	C	C	C	C	C	C
2245	**E**	■	C	C	C	C	C	C	C	C	C	C	C	C	C	C	C	C	C	C	C	C	C	C	C	C	C	C	C	C	C	C	C

Car Ferry Tariffs

Motorist Fares/Vehicle Rates for Single Journeys

Motorist Fares (driver and accompanying passengers)	**Tariff E** £	**Tariff D** £	**Tariff C** £	**Tariff B** £
Adult	11.00	11.00	11.00	11.00
Child (4 but under 14 years)	5.50	5.50	5.50	5.50
Vehicle Rates Cars, Motorised Caravans, Minibuses and Three-wheeled Vehicles				
Up to 4.00m in length	18.00	29.00	39.00	49.00
Up to 5.50m in length	18.00	36.00	49.00	59.00
Over 5.00m: each additional metre (or part thereof)	9.00	9.00	9.00	9.00
Caravans/Trailers				
Up to 5.50m in length	10.00	20.00	10.00	FREE
Over 5.50m: each additional metre (or part thereof)	10.00	10.00	10.00	FREE
Motorcycles/Scooters	8.00	10.00	11.00	12.00
Bicycles/Tandems	FREE	FREE	FREE	FREE
Cyclists pay foot passenger fare				

Foot Passenger Fares

	ADULT	**CHILD 4 & under 14**
Single	£13.00	£7.00
60 Hour Excursion (Return)	£15.50	£9.30
5 Day (120 Hours) Excursion (Return)	£20.50	£14.00

Writing for a purpose

1 **a** Imagine you work for a travel agency and take a phone call from a client who asks you to make cross-Channel ferry bookings for him. These are the details he provides:

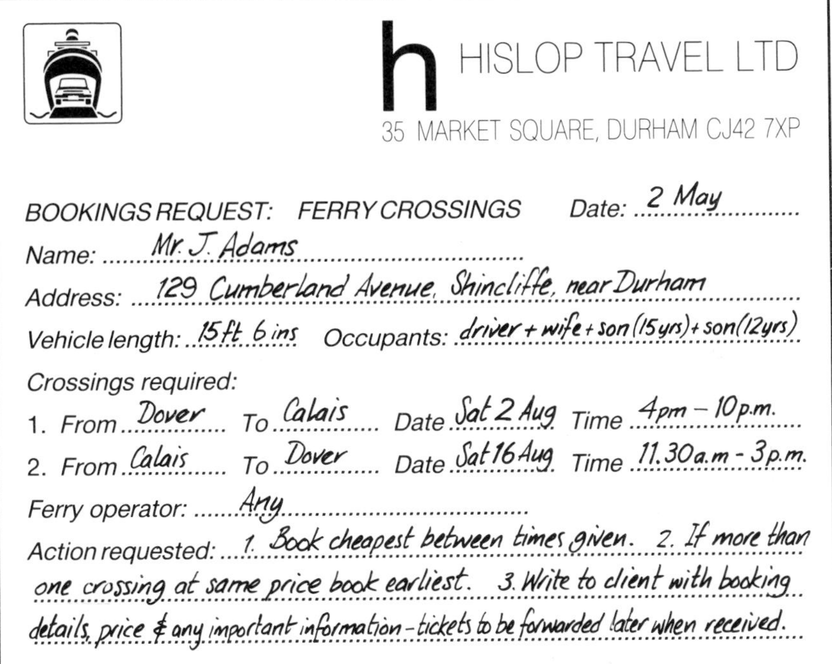

HISLOP TRAVEL LTD

35 MARKET SQUARE, DURHAM CJ42 7XP

BOOKINGS REQUEST: FERRY CROSSINGS Date: 2 May

Name: Mr J. Adams

Address: 129 Cumberland Avenue, Shincliffe, near Durham

Vehicle length: 15 ft 6 ins Occupants: driver + wife + son (15 yrs) + son (12 yrs)

Crossings required:

1. From Dover To Calais Date Sat 2 Aug Time 4pm – 10p.m.
2. From Calais To Dover Date Sat 16 Aug Time 11.30a.m - 3p.m.

Ferry operator: Any

Action requested: 1. Book cheapest between times given. 2. If more than one crossing at same price book earliest. 3. Write to client with booking details, price & any important information - tickets to be forwarded later when received.

Using the extracts from the Sealink brochure, decide which crossings would meet Mr Adams' requirements, and then, assuming you have made the bookings, write to him with the information he has requested.

b Mr Adams intends to break the long drive down to Dover by spending the night before the crossing in London. He sees this newspaper advertisement:

bfast. Special wkly bargains £95 p.p. incl. VAT. 01-584 2038.

ERITH HOTEL 24 Girton Place W2. Col. TV & bath all rooms. Lic'd restrnt. B&B (incl. VAT): £11 sgle, £17 dble (twin or dble beds). 10% deposit with bookings plse. 01-723 7503.

London Comfortable fmly hotel, close West End. Priv. baths &

Write a letter Mr Adams could send to the Erith Hotel, making the cheapest booking that would answer his needs.

(See Resource 9, page 102.)

2 The following are situations which require the writing of a formal letter. Choose one of them.

a Some friends and yourself intend to organise a disco and will need to hire a local church hall. You write to the church in question to make the booking, realising that they will require details of the use to which the hall is to be put before they will agree to let you hire it.

b A club to which you belong wants to arrange a meeting at which a well-known person comes to speak; you are given the job of writing to invite the celebrity. You should provide some information about the club and indicate what sort of thing you would like him or her to talk about, whether you would meet travel expenses and which would be the most suitable dates.

c Your class has planned an outing to places of interest in the area and transport will be needed. You write to a local coach-hire firm, outlining your requirements – the date of the excursion, size of coach, places to be visited – and asking whether they are prepared to take the job and what they would charge.

(See Resource 9, page 102.)

Other writing

Holiday of a Lifetime

Imagine you have won a holiday, all expenses paid: you are allowed to choose three places anywhere in the world and will be taken to spend a week at each. Make your choice, selecting three destinations very different from each other, and explain clearly what attracts you to them and how you imagine spending your time when you are there.

12 Articles for school magazines

A brave experiment

Wednesday December 16th

I am in an experimental Nativity play at school. It is called *Manger to Star*. I am playing Joseph. Pandora is playing Mary. Jesus is played by the smallest first-year. He is called Peter Brown. He is on drugs to make him taller.

Friday December 18th

Today's rehearsal of *Manger to Star* was a fiasco. Peter Brown has grown too big for the crib, so Mr Animbo, the Woodwork teacher, has got to make another one.

The headmaster sat at the back of the gym and watched rehearsals. He had a face like the north face of the Eiger by the time we'd got to the bit where the three wise men were accused of being capitalist pigs.

He took Miss Elf into the showers and had a 'Quiet Word'. We all heard every word he shouted. He said he wanted to see a traditional Nativity play, with a Tiny Tears doll playing Jesus and three wise men dressed in dressing gowns and tea towels. He threatened to cancel the play if Mary, alias Pandora, continued to pretend to go into labour in the manger. This is typical of Scruton – he is nothing but a small-minded, sexually-inhibited fascist pig. How he rose to become a headmaster I do not know. How can we change it now? The play is being performed on Tuesday afternoon.

Sunday December 20th

Pandora and I had a private Mary and Joseph rehearsal in my bedroom. We improvised a great scene where Mary gets back from the Family Planning Clinic and tells Joseph she's pregnant. It was dead good until my father complained about the shouting.

Tuesday December 22nd

The school concert was not a success. The bell ringing from class One-G went on too long, my father said, 'The Bells! The Bells!' and my mother laughed too loudly and made Mr Scruton look at her.

The school orchestra was a disaster! My mother said, 'When are they going to stop tuning-up and start playing?' I told her that they had just played a Mozart horn concerto. That made my mother and father and Pandora's mother and father start laughing in a very unmannerly fashion. When ten-stone Alice Bernard from Three-C came on stage in a tutu and did the dying swan I thought my mother would explode. Alice Bernard's mother led the applause, but not many people followed.

The Dumbo class got up and sang a few boring old carols. Barry Kent sang all the vulgar versions (I know because I was watching his lips) then they sat down cross-legged, and brain-box Henderson from Five-K played a trumpet, Jew's harp, piano and guitar. The smarmy git looked dead superior when he was bowing during his applause. Then it was the interval and time for me to change into my white T-shirt-and-Wranglers Joseph costume. The tension back-stage was electric. I stood in the wings and watched the audience filing back into their places. Then the music from *Close Encounters* boomed out over the stereo speakers, and the curtains opened on an abstract manger and I just had time to whisper to Pandora, 'Break a leg, darling', before Miss Elf pushed us out into the lights. My performance was brilliant! I really got under the skin of Joseph but Pandora was less good – she forgot to look tenderly at Jesus/Peter Brown.

The three punks/wise men made too much noise with their chains and spoiled my speech about the Middle East situation, and the angels representing Mrs Thatcher got hissed by the audience so loudly that their spoken chorus about unemployment was wasted.

Still, all in all, it was well received by the audience. Mr Scruton got up and made a hypocritical speech about 'a brave experiment' and 'Miss Elf's tireless work behind the scenes', and then we all sang 'We wish you a Merry Christmas'!

Driving home in the car my father said, 'That was the funniest Nativity play I have ever seen. Whose idea was it to turn it into a comedy?' I didn't reply. It wasn't a comedy.

SUE TOWNSEND
The Secret Diary of Adrian Mole Aged 13¾

Writing for a purpose

1 You have the difficult job of writing a review in fewer than 250 words of this unfortunate concert and Nativity play for the school magazine. You probably know that such articles try to give a generally favourable impression of the event they are reporting – after all, the school has its reputation to consider! You should therefore approach your task in a generous frame of mind, praising wherever possible and expressing in a very mild way any criticisms you feel you must make.

2 Write one of the following articles for the school magazine:
   a an account of a trip or holiday you have taken with the school recently;
   b a report of the activities during the past few weeks of a school society to which you belong;
   c an editorial which reviews whatever has happened of interest in the life of the school in recent months.

Other writing

In the Limelight
All of us have at some time performed, perhaps against our will, in front of an audience, in a play, concert, procession or display, for example – occasions which are often happier to look back on than actually to live through. Write about one or more such experiences you have had, trying to communicate your feelings before, during and immediately after the event.

A Gala Evening
If you could choose half a dozen performers of different sorts to take part in a charity concert that would attract a large audience representing a range of age groups and interests, who would they be? Justify each of your choices in turn, explaining why you consider them to be excellent entertainers in themselves and how each would help widen the appeal of the concert.

13 Personal letters to persuade

Taste for adventure

PGL's PREMIER ADVENTURE HOLIDAY

Windsurfing, Sailing, Canoeing – This is . . .

Sunsport.

SUNSPORT is a unique adventure holiday. The formula for perfection has been carefully developed over the years to the point where we can now proudly say that no other holiday, whatever the cost, can compare in terms of excitement and achievement. On a Sunsport holiday, **anyone** can master the basics of windsurfing, sailing and Canadian canoeing, whilst still enjoying to the full the spectacular scenery and unbeatable climate of the South of France.

IN A NUTSHELL . . . Sunsport is an all-inclusive 10 or 15 day holiday spent at two different locations in the South of France. The first half is spent beside the Mediterranean, getting to grips with sailing and windsurfing, whilst the second half is spent 100 miles inland, deep in the Ardeche Gorge, tackling the Ardeche river by Canadian canoe. All the equipment needed for the above activities is provided, as well as full and continuous instruction and supervision. A complete programme of dry land activities and evening entertainments takes over whenever you are not on the water.

WHO CAN DO IT? Virtually anybody! We have four separate departures, to cater for 12–15 year olds, 16–18 year olds, families and 18 plus. No previous experience of any of the sports is required, but all guests must be able to swim 50 metres. All activities are arranged with safety in mind and buoyancy aids are provided. Each group of between 35 and 45 people combine to form a "battalion", ready to tackle what, for many, is their first real taste of adventure.

WATERSPORTS ON THE MEDITERRANEAN

There is no feeling like waking up to another morning of sunshine, blue skies, sandy beaches and warm seas. You want to get in or on the water and the PGL programme allows you to do just that.

Windsurfing continues to grow in popularity and indeed, it is now an Olympic sport. Our experienced instructors not only give you initial instruction but will constantly monitor your progress over the whole holiday. Slow learners will be encouraged, whilst those who find they have the "knack" will be given plenty of scope and tuition in order to develop their skills.

Our easy-to-sail Topper dinghies with their simple single sail are ideal to learn in, but still responsive and fun to sail. It only takes a short period of dry land instruction before you are afloat on the Mediterranean, putting theory into practice. Instruction and supervision continue from accompanying dinghies and the rescue boat, as you sail in pairs or later single-handed if you're up to it and willing.

Naturally enough, many of the evening's entertainments are centred on the beach and may include fancy dress, five-a-side football, barbecues and It's-a-Knockout. Further possibilities are staff reviews and talent shows, held in the marquee.

Our Sunsport Mediterranean centres are located on the wide sandy beaches of the Languedoc coast near Beziers. With the development of tourism in the area over the last decade, many modern campsites have been established on the very fringes of the beach. We have hired sections on two of these and established our own little "villages" for our holidaymakers.

Accommodation is in 2 berth tents with foam mattresses and sleeping bags provided.

CANOEING ON THE ARDECHE The Ardeche River is relatively unknown in Britain yet it is among the greatest scenic attractions of Europe. For some 30 kilometres it has cut a winding course through the limestone edge of the Massif Central forming a magnificent wooded canyon 600 feet deep.

Canoeists from all over Europe come to test their skills on this river which experienced canoeists find satisfying and novices find challenging. Yet none of the rapids are too demanding, nor any of the calm stretches too long. It is for these reasons that the Ardeche is unique among the rivers of Europe.

It is impossible to describe the exhilaration, the excitement, the enjoyment and the satisfaction of the canoe descent. Only by experiencing its challenge can it be fully appreciated.

We use tough, safe, 2-person Canadian canoes, with instructors who are chosen for their personalities as well as their qualifications and experience. The descent is at a leisurely pace with time to run the rapids again and again.

Evening entertainments in the Ardeche make the most of its wooded location. Activities may include such things as treasure trails, orienteering, table tennis and volleyball tournaments, discos, pop quizzes and bar games based on TV programmes such as "Give Us a Clue".

We have two centres in the Ardeche, both close to the river. Le Mas de Serret is most magnificently situated above the Ardeche gorge itself with views across the surrounding countryside. It is a converted hunting lodge set in its own wooded grounds, and, incidentally, was used by the French Resistance during the Second World War. Accommodation is in modern 2-berth tents grouped in clearings. In and around the courtyard and its attractive rough stone buildings are the toilet/shower facilities, the dining room and the bar/disco.

Chataigneraie is beautifully located in wooded grounds running down to the beaches bordering the Ardeche. Massive limestone cliffs rise high above it, creating an unequalled sense of grandeur and tranquility.

Accommodation is in tents with all other facilities in permanent buildings.

10-DAY ITINERARY

(This sample itinerary visits the Ardeche centre first, but some holidays will commence at the Mediterranean.)

Day 1
Early afternoon departure from central London to connect with ferry crossing to Calais. A luxury coach travels onwards through the night arriving on the Ardeche at approximately 10.00a.m. on Day 2.

Day 2
Relaxing afternoon, learning how to handle the Canadian canoes, plus time for swimming.

Day 3
A short visit to the town of Vallon before tackling the first stretch of the river from Vallon to La Chataigneraie.

Day 4
This activity day gives you a choice of swimming, caving, walking or advanced canoeing.

Day 5
Canoeing through spectacular scenery from La Chataigneraie to St. Martin.

Day 6
Morning transfer by coach to the Mediterranean centre and afternoon at leisure on the beach. Introduction to windsurfing.

Day 7
Windsurfing in the morning, followed by an introduction to topper sailing in the afternoon.

Day 8
Full day excursion, either by coach or longboat – choice of destinations including the fabulous waterpark, AQUALAND.

Day 9
Last chance to perfect your windsurfing and sailing. Leave by coach late afternoon on the homeward journey to the Channel.

Day 10
Early morning ferry connects with coach in Dover. Estimated arrival time in central London is 13.00 hours.

PRICES & DEPARTURES Sunsport

BOOKING CODES	FR2	FR3	FR5	FR6
Holiday	15 days	10 days	15 days	10 days
Age Range	12–15	12–15	16–18	16–18
COMMENCING DATES				
August 4	**£329**	–	–	–
July 7, 14, 21, 28, August 4, 11, 18	–	**£229**	–	**£229**
July 14, 21	–	–	**£329**	–

Writing for a purpose

1 You and a friend have decided you will take a holiday together in the summer. You will have saved about £300 each and your friend seems quite keen on ten days soaking up the sun on a Spanish beach. However, you would prefer something more active and the Sunsport adventure holiday appeals to you, though neither of you has tried the activities included in the holiday before.

Write a letter to your friend, proposing the idea. Taking your information from the advertisement, describe the attractive features of the holiday in a way that you think will persuade your reader to share your enthusiasm and meet any objections he or she might have.

2 Write a letter in which you attempt to do one of the following:

a encourage a penfriend to come to stay with you for a while, describing what there is to do and see that would make the holiday enjoyable;

b persuade a friend to take up some leisure pursuit which already gives you a good deal of pleasure;

c dissuade a friend from a course of action he or she is considering but which you feel would be unwise; for example, leaving school before sitting the GCSE exams, joining an organisation of which you disapprove, taking up a career you think unsuitable, leaving home to live in rented accommodation. You need to choose your arguments very carefully and present them tactfully so that you do not give offence.

Other writing

Living Dangerously

Most of us find adventure in one form or another enjoyable, but young people sometimes complain that modern living is very tame: nearly all our activities are organised for us, predictable and boringly safe. What are your own views on the matter? How much danger do we really want in our lives? Is there in fact so little scope for adventure and excitement nowadays?

14 Newspaper articles

A table for two

Miss Elizabeth Mapp and Mrs Emmeline ('Lucia') Lucas were leading lights in Tilling society and deadly rivals. On this occasion Elizabeth had made her way to Lucia's house, Grebe Cottage, a little way out of town and beside a dyke protecting it from the river swollen by recent storms. She had slipped unseen into the kitchen in search of Lucia's closely guarded recipe for lobster and had found it when:

She heard with a sudden stoppage of her heart-beat, a step on the crisp path outside, and the handle of the kitchen-door was turned. Elizabeth took one sideways stride behind the gaudy tree and, peering through its branches, saw Lucia standing at the entrance. Lucia came straight towards her, not yet perceiving that there was a Boxing Day burglar in her own kitchen, and stood admiring her tree. Then with a startled exclamation she called out, 'Who's there?' and Elizabeth knew that she was discovered. Further dodging behind the decorated fir would be both undignified and ineffectual, however skilful her footwork.

'It's me, dear Lucia,' she said. 'I came to thank you in person for the delicious *pâté* and to ask if –'

From somewhere close outside there came a terrific roar and rush as of great water-floods released. Reunited for the moment by a startled curiosity, they ran together to the open door, and saw, already leaping across the road and over the hornbeam hedge, a solid wall of water.

'The bank has given way,' cried Lucia. 'Quick, into the house through the door in the kitchen, and up the stairs.'

They fled back past the Christmas tree, and tried the door into the house. It was locked: the servants had evidently taken this precaution before going out on their pleasuring.

'We shall be drowned,' wailed Elizabeth, as the flood came foaming into the kitchen.

'Rubbish,' cried Lucia. 'The kitchen-table! We must turn it upside down and get onto it.'

It was but the work of a moment to do this, for the table was already on its side, and the two stepped over the high boarding that ran round it. Would their weight be too great to allow it to float on the rushing water that now deepened rapidly in the kitchen? That anxiety was short-lived, for it rose free from the floor and bumped gently into the Christmas tree.

'We must get out of this,' cried Lucia. 'One doesn't know how much the water will rise. We may be drowned yet if the table legs come against the ceiling. Catch hold of the dresser and pull.'

But there was no need for such exertion, for the flood, eddying fiercely round the submerged kitchen, took them out of the doors that had been flung wide, and in a few minutes they were floating away over the garden and the hornbeam hedge. The tide had evidently begun to ebb before the bank gave way, and now the kitchen-table, occasionally turning round in an eddy, moved off in the direction of Tilling and of the sea. Luckily it had not got into the main stream of the river but floated smoothly and swiftly along, with the tide and the torrent to carry it.

From the high ground on which Tilling stood, a group of Elizabeth and Lucia's friends had been looking out over the fields below them when the dyke burst.

All but Georgie had heard the rush and roar of the released waters, but his eyes were sharper than others, and he had been the first to see where the disaster had occurred.

'Look, the bank opposite Grebe has burst!' he cried. 'The road's under water, her garden's under water: the rooms downstairs must be flooded. I hope Lucia's upstairs, or she'll get dreadfully wet.'

'And that road is Elizabeth's favourite walk,' cried Diva. 'She'll be on it now.'

'But she walks so fast,' said the Padre, forgetting to speak Scotch. 'She'll be past Grebe by now, and above where the bank has burst.'

'Oh dear, oh dear, and on Boxing Day!' wailed Mrs Bartlett.

The huge flood was fast advancing on the town, but with this outlet over the fields, it was evident that it would get no deeper at Grebe, and that, given Lucia was upstairs and that Elizabeth had walked as fast as usual, there was no real anxiety for them. All eyes now watched the progress of the water. It rose like a wave over a rock when it came to the railway line that crossed the marsh and in a couple of minutes more it was foaming over the fields immediately below the town.

Again Georgie uttered woe like Cassandra.

'There's something coming,' he cried. 'It looks like a raft with its legs in the air. And there are two people on it. Now it's spinning round and round; now it's coming straight here ever so fast. There are two women, one without a hat. It's Them! It's Lucia and Miss Mapp! What *has* happened?'

The raft, with legs sometimes madly waltzing, sometimes floating smoothly along, was borne swiftly towards the bottom of the cliff, below which the flood was pouring by. The Padre, with his new umbrella, ran down the steps that led to the road below in order to hook it in, if it approached within umbrella-distance. On and on it came, now clearly recognisable as Lucia's great kitchen-table upside down, until it was within a yard or two of the bank. To attempt to wade out to it, for any effective purpose, was useless: the strongest would be swept away in such a headlong torrent, and even if he reached the raft there would be three helpless people on it instead of two and it would probably sink. To hook it with the umbrella was the only chance, for there was no time to get a boat-hook or a rope to throw out to the passengers. The Padre made a desperate lunge at it, slipped and fell flat into the water, and was only saved from being carried away by clutching at the iron railing alongside the lowest of the submerged steps. Then some fresh current tweaked the table and, still moving in the general direction of the flood water, it sheered off across the fields. As it receded Lucia showed the real stuff of which she was made. She waved her hand and her clear voice rang out gaily across the waste of water.

'Au reservoir, all of you,' she cried. 'We'll come back: just wait till we come back,' and she was seen to put her arm round the huddled form of Mapp, and comfort her.

The kitchen-table was observed by the watchers to get into the main channel of the river, where the water was swifter yet. It twirled round once or twice as if waving farewell, and then shot off towards the sea and that great bank of thick mist which hung over the horizon.

E F BENSON
Mapp and Lucia

Writing for a purpose

1 Use the information in the passage as the basis of a news article to appear in the next edition of *The Tilling Gazette*. You are free to invent additional material – for example, the organisation of a sea search – and you should include in your article at least one interview with someone involved – perhaps the Padre, the coastguard or the ladies themselves if they have been rescued by the time the newspaper goes to press. Choose a suitably strik-

ing headline and assume that the editor has limited you to no more than 300 words. (See Resource 10, page 103.)

2 Write a newspaper article which has one of these headlines:

Youngsters' Outing Turns to Nightmare
Teacher Runs Amok in Classroom Rumpus
Police End Family's Gunpoint Ordeal
Rescue Drama: Teenager's Courage Praised
Pupil Prank Closes Local School

(See Resource 10, page 103.)

Other writing

Daggers Drawn
In the extract, despite their rivalry, Mapp and Lucia are united by circumstances – at least for a while. Write a short story which takes the rivalry of two individuals or groups as its theme, perhaps developing a situation which eventually draws the warring parties together.

15 Situation reports in letter form

Saltash Bridge

W HEATH ROBINSON *The Building of Saltash Bridge*

Writing for a purpose

1 The Saltash Bridge is being built by Heath Robinson Construction Ltd for the Government Department of Transport. Imagine you are an inspector for that department and, having visited the site to check on progress, you write a report in the form of a letter which you send to the construction firm. It is clear that you are not at all happy with what you saw.

After a short introductory paragraph, organise your findings under these headings:

Method of construction
Safety standards
Overstaffing and inefficient use of labour
Conclusions

(See Resource 11, page 104.)

2 The Parents Association of your school is taking an interest in one of the following:

a the school's dining arrangements;
b the opportunities the school offers pupils to develop out-of-class interests in music, sport, drama and so forth;
c what the school is contributing to the life of the local community through, for example, voluntary social work, evening events open to the public and so on;
d what measures the school takes to encourage first-year pupils to settle in quickly and painlessly.

The Secretary of the Association asks the school to provide details of present arrangements and to comment on whether these are felt to be satisfactory. You are given the job of replying in writing to the Secretary. Produce a report in letter form, giving the information requested under whatever headings seem appropriate. (See Resource 11, page 104.)

Other Writing

One of Those Days

Site manager for the building of the Saltash Bridge cannot be an easy job! Write an account of an hour or two in this unfortunate individual's working day during which he or she struggles to cope with mounting chaos.

16 Application letters and *curricula vitae*

Write for the job

As a way of getting her to think seriously about her future and to bring together information she might want to include in later applications, Jennifer, like other fifth-formers intending to leave at the end of the year, was asked by her careers teacher to fill in a questionnaire:

Fenborough Secondary School

Full name: Jennifer Karen Preston Form: 5J

Home Address: 14 Tower Close, Fenborough

GCSE subjects you hope to take this summer: English, Maths Biology, History, French, Domestic Science, Art

Which of these do you enjoy most? Biology, Maths

Which do you expect to do best in? Biology, English, Domestic Science

---

Out-of-class activities, including responsibilities: Duke of Edinburgh (working for Bronze Award), Natural History Soc. (Treasurer), school netball team, last school play (backstage)

Any school responsibilities not covered above: 4th form games captain

---

Out-of-school interests: My dogs (all three !!), horse-riding, badminton, swimming, writing to foreign pen-friends, discos

Work experience: Saturday and holiday job at Alkhurst Kennels

Any other useful experience or achievements: Member of St John Ambulance

---

Type of permanent work that would interest you: Something with animals - otherwise perhaps catering or hotel work

Would you agree to further study as part of your work? Yes

Have you already done anything about finding a job? If so, what? No

Has anyone outside school agreed to write you a reference? If so, give name, address and position: Mrs H Bennetts, Alkhurst Kennels, Priory Lane, Hawkley, Fenborough. (Owner)

Writing for a purpose

1 Later Jennifer sees this advertisement in *The Fenborough Herald*:

> Wanted
> **GIRL FRIDAY**
>
> A busy veterinary practice requires a young person, enthusiastic and of smart appearance, for reception and general duties. Excellent opportunity for a school-leaver wishing eventually to qualify as animal nursing auxiliary through home-study and day release.
>
> Apply in writing to:
> J H Fenton, Veterinary Surgeon,
> 137 Westbrooke Street, Fenborough.

She is keen to apply. Judging from the information she gives in some of her answers to the questionnaire, the job and its prospects would suit Jennifer very well, but she will only be invited to an interview if she is able to present this information strongly in her letter and create a favourable general impression of herself.

Write your own version of Jennifer's letter, bearing in mind that not all the details she has provided on the questionnaire will be relevant to this application. (See Resource 12, page 105.)

2 **a** Invent a newspaper advertisement for the sort of job that would interest you if you left school at the end of the fifth year and which you could realistically hope to get. Then write a letter of application. (See Resource 12, page 105.)

b Sometimes a job-application will take the form of a sheet summarising one's personal details, qualifications, interests and so forth, which is called a *curriculum vitae* or CV. This is sent together with a covering letter which draws attention to whatever in the CV is particularly relevant to the application and tries to convey a confident, enthusiastic attitude towards the type of work in question. Reply to the advertisement you produced for the first part of this exercise with your CV and an accompanying letter. (See Resource 13, pages 106 and 107.)

Other writing

When I Grow Up

Some people seem to know from a very early age exactly what career they eventually want to follow and are quite clear why; others go through an often unrealistic catalogue of ambitions before they finally make up their minds; still others never properly decide what job would really suit them – though they are usually very sure what types of work they would hate. How has it been in your own case? What are your own thoughts and feelings on the subject of employment?

Level three

17 Advertising material

Sinclair's electric buggy

On 10th January, 1985 Sir Clive Sinclair, pioneer in the field of pocket calculators, home computers and miniature televisions, launched his electric pedal car. The next day this editorial appeared in The Times:

Loophole wagon

The search for the practicable electric car has been like the search for the Philosopher's Stone through almost the whole of the hundred-year history of the motor car. Electric power is quiet, pollution-free and in principle cheaper than setting fire to refined vapours in confined spaces and converting the blast into rotary motion. Manufacturers all over the world have for ever been tantalisingly on the edge of a breakthrough, but have always foundered on the problem of storage. Conventional lead-acid batteries are heavy and expensive, and do not stand up long to the power demands of normal driving without frequent recharging.

If Sir Clive Sinclair can master this problem, he will be a benefactor of mankind and will deserve to reap the rewards of his undoubted ingenuity and enterprise. But it does not appear that he has done so yet. Inventive though it is in many details, his company's new car (tricycle? pedal dodgem? – a new name is called for) uses conventional batteries and is handicapped in speed and range like its predecessors, though allegedly extremely cheap to operate. It does not pretend to do a car's job. In price and capacity, it is closest to the moped bicycle, which has a better turn of speed but has never enjoyed more than moderate favour in the British climate.

It is in fact a loophole vehicle, devised to take advantage of changes made in the law in 1983. Since then it has been possible to run small electric vehicles on the highway without road tax, licence or compulsory insurance. In theory, there are many advantages in machines which take up so little room on the road and in the car park, which spread no fumes and are incapable of that burst of bad-tempered speed which leads to so many accidents. One of the great absurdities of our day is the spectacle of rush-hour traffic, with family cars three abreast, powerful engines expensively idling, each one with just one person in (and buses with 30 passengers aboard wedged deep in the crush). It will be interesting to see the effect of large numbers of Sinclair buggies released into the scene, compact, odourless, but possibly disruptively different in their driving characteristics (perhaps generating as many queues as milk-floats) and free to park anywhere, regardless of yellow lines, meters or wheel-clamps.

The prospect gives reason for concern as well as curiosity. It is hard to predict how safe such a vehicle will be in heavy traffic, when anyone over 14 will be free to drive it without test or insurance. It is true that its speed will not be much greater than that of a push-bike, which children may ride on the open road – and do, often at some danger to themselves and others. The new machine is likely to be less dangerous than most motor-bicycles, but this is not saying much in a category which is involved in a quarter of all fatal accidents though it accounts for only three per cent of motor mileage. More than half of the motorcyclists killed on the roads are aged between 17 and 20. If an uninsured buggy does cause an accident, who will pay? Exempt from safeguards regarded as necessary for most other powered vehicles, the loophole wagon will deserve very close watching in its early months to ensure that the exemptions are not harmful.

Writing for a purpose

1 Imagine you were asked to produce a large newspaper advertisement for the C5 or a publicity leaflet of the sort dealers give their customers to promote sales. Go through the editorial and the list of specifications on page 60, deciding which features of the vehicle were its most promising selling points and how best to present them.

In fact the C5 was not a success: advance publicity led the public to expect too much, some of the misgivings expressed in the editorial were never properly put to rest and, in general, the vehicle failed to gain 'an acceptable image' – people seemed to treat it as a sort of joke. You should bear these facts in mind when you consider what might have been an effective way of promoting the product, a way that might have won a more favourable response from the public.

Your aim is to convey your information forcefully and attractively; and since the impact of an advertisement depends partly on how it *looks*, lay out your work as you would want it printed, indicating where an illustration of the C5 would be placed. (See Resource 20, pages 116–118.)

SINCLAIR C5	
Price:	£399.
Retail outlets:	electricity board showrooms; mail order; chain stores.
Dimensions:	length 5′9″ (174 cm); width 2′5″ (74 cm); height 2′7″ (79.5 cm).
Weight:	66 lbs + battery 33 lbs.
Luggage capacity:	22 lbs (1 cu. ft)
Construction:	steel chassis; aerodynamic polypropylene body (light, strong, resilient, rust-free); reinforced nylon wheels (pneumatic).
Controls:	comfortably positioned handlebars; off/on acceleration button; no clutch or gears.
Battery:	rechargeable in 8 hrs from flat hundreds of times; recharger included in price.
Range:	up to 20 miles (double if second battery carried) at less than ¼p a mile; pedals in case of emergency.
Maximum speed:	15 mph.
The Law:	no licence, insurance, road tax or helmet required; minimum age 14.
Parking:	restrictions do not apply; 5 C5s can be parked in space needed for one family saloon.
Optional Accessories:	designer-styled weatherproof cover; side panels; mud-flaps; wing-mirrors; high-visibility mast; indicators; horn; seat cushions; seat booster for smaller drivers.
Servicing:	by Hoover engineers, at owner's home if desired.

2 Produce a leaflet or newspaper advertisement of the kind described in Exercise 1, promoting one of the following:

a a product with which you are familiar – for example, a certain bicycle, piece of sports equipment, portable radio, calculator, digital watch – or one of the inventions illustrated in Unit 3.

b a particular occupation as a worthwhile career; for example, nursing, the armed forces or police, hairdressing, teaching, farming;

c your own area or one you know well, as a tourist or holiday centre;

d a local amenity – for example, a sports centre, library, theatre, museum.

(See Resource 20, pages 116–118.)

Other writing

The Motor Vehicle: Curse or Blessing?
The petrol engine is certainly one of the most important inventions of modern times: it has transformed life – not always for the better. Discuss the benefit and the harm for which motor vehicles are responsible, connecting and developing your material so as to avoid producing a mere list of disjointed points. In your final paragraph, consider how, on balance, you would answer the question in the title.

The Shape of Things to Come
Means of travel are, of course, only one of the areas of our lives which will probably be revolutionised during the coming years. Write about your average day thirty years from now to give some idea of how different you imagine life will be then. You may present your work in the form of a diary entry if you wish.

18 Debate speeches

Anyone for marriage?

Writing for a purpose

1 Organised debates are designed to avoid the pointless free-for-alls that can develop when people find themselves strongly disagreeing on some question. They are rather formal occasions organised according to quite strict rules which your teacher may want to describe to you.

Consider the comments on marriage made on the opposite page, decide which side you would opt for if you had to choose one or the other, and then write a debate speech either supporting or opposing the view: *Marriage is an outdated institution which has no place in a sensible society*. Your speech should take five minutes or so to deliver and you may make use of any additional ideas you might have on the subject. (See Resource 2, page 94 and Resource 14, page 108.)

2 Write a debate speech, about five minutes long, on some issue that interests you. If you are short of ideas for a topic, you could choose to support or oppose one of these opinions:

a a woman's place is in the home;
b schools today offer their pupils a poor preparation for later life;
c on the whole progress has reduced human happiness, not increased it;
d money spent on research in space is money wasted;
e it is time trade unions were abolished.

(See Resource 2, page 94 and Resource 14, page 108.)

Other writing

A Storm in a Teacup
What begins as a good-natured difference of opinion amongst friends can easily become a heated, unpleasant affair, leaving those who took part upset and bewildered about how it all happened. Write an account of such an argument which gets out of hand, presenting your work as a play if you wish.

Happy Families
Write an essay in which you consider the attitudes and qualities which are needed in the members of a family if they are to get on well together.

19 Reports making comparisons

Snap decision

YESHIBA JUNIOR
35mm COMPACT CAMERA

Size: .... 4½ × 2¾ × 1½in.
Film:............... spool, rather 'fiddly' to insert.
Operation: .... no focusing necessary; simple light-setting with symbols.
Flash: .... built in.
Slides:............. choice of slides or prints.
Picture quality:... good.
Special features:. *light indicates when flash is charged and ready to fire.
*pouch case.
Prices:............. Camera, £27 approx.
Film, £1.90 approx for 24 exposures.

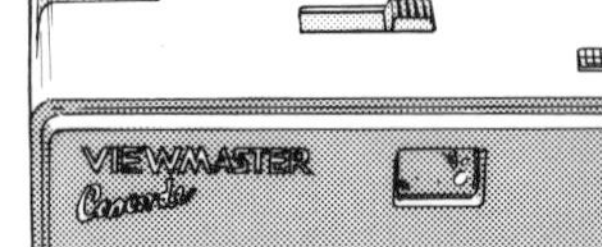

VIEWMASTER CONCORDE
110 POCKET CAMERA

Size: .... 6 × 1 × 2¼in.
Film:............... easy-loading cartridge.
Operation: .... no focusing needed; camera adjusts automatically to light conditions.
Flash: .... built in.
Slides:............. not possible, prints only.
Picture quality:... produces smaller negatives than the 35mm camera so prints are not quite as sharp and detailed.
Special features:. *low-light signal indicates when flash is necessary.
*film winds on automatically.
*choice of normal lens or telephoto for close-ups.
Prices:............. Camera, £28 approx.
Film, £2 approx for 24 exposures.

INSTAPRINT 300
INSTANT PICTURE CAMERA

Size: .... folds down to $7\frac{1}{2} \times 6\frac{1}{4} \times 2\frac{1}{2}$in.
Film:................ easy-loading cartridge.
Operation: .... no focusing necessary; camera adjusts automatically to light conditions, though some manual adjustment is possible.
Flash: .... built in; fires whenever camera is used, whether needed or not.
Slides:.............. not possible, prints only.
Picture quality:... reasonably good but colours can be disappointing.
Special feature: .. *print delivered immediately and develops itself in seconds.
Prices:.............. Camera, £30 approx.
Film, £7 approx for 10 prints (flash batteries included).

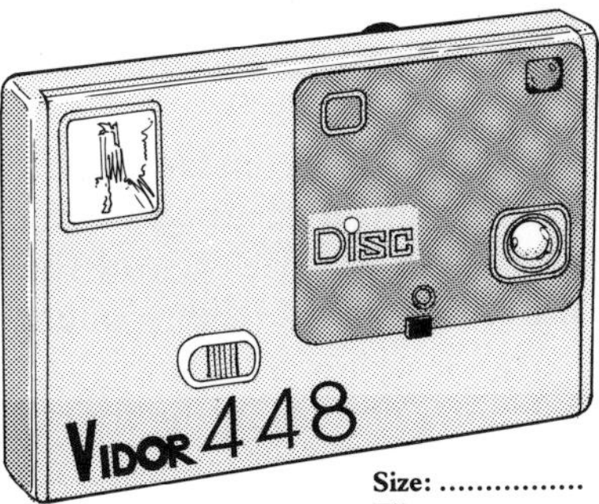

VIDOR 448
DISC CAMERA

Size: .... $4\frac{1}{2} \times 3 \times \frac{3}{4}$in.
Film:................ easy-loading disc.
Operation: .... no focusing needed; camera adjusts automatically to light conditions.
Flash: .... built in.
Slides:.............. not possible, prints only.
Picture quality:... produces very small negatives so pictures tend to be 'grainy' and not very sharp.
Special features: . *flash operates automatically but only when needed.
*film winds on automatically.
*sliding lens cover when camera not in use.
*wrist-strap.
Prices:.............. Camera, £29 approx.
Film, £1.90 approx for 15 exposures.

Writing for a purpose

1 Imagine that a member of your class is moving from the area and therefore leaving the school. The class want to buy this person a surprise farewell present and happen to know he/she would like a camera – something uncomplicated but reliable, mainly for taking holiday snaps. In a fit of generosity £30 is raised and you are given the task of looking into what types of camera are available for the price and suggesting which would be the most suitable for the boy or girl in question.

You do the job very thoroughly, obtaining information on the four types of camera (see pages 64 and 65) and then writing a report in which you consider the advantages and drawbacks of each camera in turn and make a final recommendation. (See Resource 15, page 109.)

2 Write one of the following reports:

a after a fund-raising event, a school has £1000 to spend in a way that will produce the most benefit for the pupils. This short-list of ideas is drawn up:

- buying a video camera and recorder, neither of which the school possesses at the moment;
- redecorating some of the classrooms which are in a very shoddy state;
- putting the money towards replacing the school minibus which is nearing the end of its days;
- giving the money to the Sports Department which is badly off for equipment.

A committee is appointed to decide which proposal should be adopted. Write the report the committee might produce, considering what is to be said for and against each of the four suggestions and then indicating which of them ought, on balance, to be chosen.

b A school intends to introduce general studies in the fourth year during a double period each week. Four courses will be timetabled – courses in subjects it is hoped will be of practical use to pupils or increase their understanding of the world in which they live – and each pupil will have to opt for a different course each term. There are staff available to teach the following for beginners:

computing; British politics and government; cookery; world religions; woodwork; typing; motor cycle and car maintenance; the problems facing developing countries.

You are invited to express in writing your views on which four of these courses should be made available to pupils. Make your choice, explaining carefully why you think the four you have selected are suitable general studies courses and briefly why you are rejecting the others.
(See Resource 15, page 109.)

Other writing

Looking Back
Old photographs can produce a strange mixture of emotions: even while we are smiling at the memories they recall, we can feel sad, for example. Imagine you are sitting with a member of your family or an old friend, looking through a photo-album. Write an account of your conversation and the thoughts and feelings prompted by the pictures or, if you wish, develop the same idea in the form of a poem.

20 Formal letters of complaint

The test

On the afternoon Marian took her second driver's test, Mrs Ericson went with her. 'It's probably better to have someone a little older with you,' Mrs Ericson said as Marian slipped into the driver's seat beside her. 'Perhaps last time your Cousin Bill made you nervous, talking too much on the way.'

'Yes, Ma'am,' Marian said in her soft, unaccented voice. 'They probably do like it better if a white person shows up with you.'

'Oh, I don't think it's that,' Mrs Ericson began, and subsided after a glance at the girl's set profile. Marian drove the car slowly through the shady suburban streets. It was one of the first hot days of June, and when they reached the boulevard they found it crowded with cars headed for the beaches.

'Do you want me to drive?' Mrs Ericson asked. 'I'll be glad to if you're feeling jumpy.' Marian shook her head. Mrs Ericson watched her dark, competent hands and wondered for the thousandth time how the house had ever managed to get along without her, or how she had lived through those earlier years when her household had been presided over by a series of slatternly white girls who had considered housework demeaning and the care of children an added insult. 'You drive beautifully, Marian,' she said. 'Now, don't think of the last time. Anybody would slide on a steep hill on a wet day like that.'

'It takes four mistakes to flunk you,' Marian said. 'I don't remember doing all the things the inspector marked down on my blank.'

'People say that they only want you to slip them a little something,' Mrs Ericson said doubtfully.

'No,' Marian said. 'That would only make it worse, Mrs Ericson. I know.'

The car turned right, at a traffic signal, into a side road and slid up to the kerb at the rear of a short line of parked cars. The inspectors had not arrived yet.

'You have the papers?' Mrs Ericson asked. Marian took them out of her bag: her learner's licence, the car registration, and her birth certificate. They settled down to the dreary business of waiting.

'It will be marvellous to have someone dependable to drive the children to school every day,' Mrs Ericson said.

Marian looked up from the list of driving requirements she had been studying. 'It'll make things simpler at the house, won't it?' she said.

'Oh, Marian,' Mrs Ericson exclaimed, 'if I could only pay you half of what you're worth!'

'Now, Mrs Ericson,' Marian said firmly. They looked at each other and smiled with affection.

Two cars with official insignia on their doors stopped across the street. The inspectors leaped out, very brisk and military in their neat uniforms. Marian's hands tightened on the wheel. 'There's the one who flunked me last time,' she whispered, pointing to a stocky, self-important man who had begun to shout directions at the driver at the head of the line. 'Oh, Mrs Ericson.'

'Now, Marian,' Mrs Ericson said. They smiled at each other again, rather weakly.

The inspector who finally reached their car was not the stocky one but a genial middle-aged man who grinned broadly as he thumbed over their papers. Mrs Ericson started to get out of the car. 'Don't you want to come along?' the inspector asked. 'Mandy and I don't mind company.'

Mrs Ericson was bewildered for a moment. 'No,' she said and stepped to the kerb. 'I might make Marian self-conscious. She's a fine driver, Inspector.'

'Sure thing,' the inspector said, winking at Mrs Ericson. He slid into the seat beside Marian. 'Turn right at the corner, Mandy-Lou.'

From the kerb, Mrs Ericson watched the car move smoothly up the street.

The inspector made notes in a small black book. 'Age?' he inquired presently, as they drove along.

'Twenty-seven.'

He looked at Marian out of the corner of his eye. 'Old enough to have quite a flock of pickaninnies, eh?'

Marian did not answer.

'Left at this corner,' the inspector said, 'and park between that truck and the green Buick.'

The two cars were very close together, but Marian squeezed in between them without too much manoeuvring. 'Driven before, Mandy-Lou?' the inspector asked.

'Yes, sir. I had a permit for three years in Pennsylvania.'*

'Why do you want to drive a car?'

* Americans are generally required to take the driving test again if they move to another state.

'My employer needs me to take her children to and from school.'

'Sure you don't really want to sneak out nights to meet some young blood?' the inspector asked. He laughed as Marian shook her head.

'Let's see you take a left at the corner and then turn around in the middle of the next block,' the inspector said. He began to whistle 'Swanee River'. 'Make you homesick?' he asked.

Marian put out her hand, swung around in the street, and headed back in the direction from which they had come. 'No,' she said. 'I was born in Scranton, Pennsylvania.'

The inspector feigned astonishment. 'You-all ain't Southern?' he said. 'Well, dog my cats if I didn't think you-all came from down yondah.'

'No, sir,' Marian said.

'Turn onto Main Street here and let's see how you-all does in heavier traffic.'

They followed a line of cars along Main Street for several blocks until they came in sight of a concrete bridge which arched high over the railway tracks.

'Read that sign at the end of the bridge,' the inspector said.

'Proceed with caution. Dangerous in slippery weather,' Marian said.

'Where d'you learn to do that, Mandy?'

'I got my college degree last year,' Marian said. Her voice was not quite steady.

As the car crept up the slope of the bridge the inspector burst out laughing. He laughed so hard he could scarcely give his direction. 'Stop here,' he said, wiping his eyes, 'then start 'er up again. Mandy got her degree, did she? Dog my cats!'

Marian pulled up beside the kerb. She put the car in neutral, pulled on the hand-brake, waited a moment, and then put the car into gear again. Her face was set. As she released the brake her foot slipped off the clutch pedal and the engine stalled.

'Now, Mistress Mandy,' the inspector said, 'remember your degree.'

'Damn you!' Marian cried. She started the car with a jerk.

The inspector lost his joviality in an instant. 'Return to the starting place, please,' he said, and made four very black crosses at random in the squares on Marian's application blank.

Mrs Ericson was waiting at the kerb where they had left her. As Marian stopped the car the inspector jumped out and brushed past her, his face purple. 'What happened?' Mrs Ericson asked, looking after him with alarm.

Marian stared down at the wheel and her lip trembled.

'Oh, Marian, again?' Mrs Ericson said.

Marian nodded. 'In a sort of different way,' she said, and slid over to the right-side of the car.

ANGELICA GIBBS
The Test

Writing for a purpose

1 Marian is obviously upset by what occurred during the test and she decides to write a letter of complaint about her treatment. She discovers that the examiner's name is Charles Hixon and that she should address her complaint to: The Director, Driver Licencing Authority, Main Street, Poynton. Write the letter Marian might have sent.

Before you begin, you should give some thought to these questions:

a What precisely has Marian got to complain of? After all, she did stall on the bridge and, as far as Mr Hixon's remarks are concerned, could he not claim he was just indulging in a little friendly 'leg-pulling'?

b How much detail is it necessary to provide? Of course, you need to support the complaint with specific information but would a long blow-by-blow account of everything said and done really be the best way of making your case?

c What are you hoping will be done? Is your concern to have Mr Hixon punished in some way, to win a fair deal for blacks in future, merely to get your qualified driver's licence or what? Realistically speaking, what could you expect the Director to agree to do?

d In a letter of this sort, what would be the most effective tone to adopt? Your first inclination might be to vent your anger in a very blunt way; would this be wise?

(See Resource 16, page 110.)

2 Write one of these letters of complaint:

a to a neighbour who keeps behaving in some unreasonable way despite your requests that he or she stop;

b to the manager of a shop where you bought some item which proved faulty and whose staff were not at all helpful when you tried to return the goods;

c to a travel firm concerning a disastrous package-holiday for which you consider you deserve compensation;

d to a headteacher from a parent who believes his or her child has been badly treated.

(See Resource 16, page 110.)

Other writing

Narrow Minds

Although we pride ourselves on being a generally tolerant society, prejudice of one type or another is by no means rare – prejudice concerning not only race but also, for example, nationality, sex, social class, appearance and age. Write either:

a a short story which features some form of prejudice; or:

b an essay in which the subject of prejudice is discussed. You might examine the problem in a general way, considering the forms prejudice takes and the reasons for it among otherwise sensible people; or you could discuss the ways you feel you personally have been victimised or indeed what your own prejudices are. Whichever approach you choose, begin by making clear exactly what you understand by the term 'prejudice' – it does not, for example, simply mean 'disapproval', does it?

21 Formal letters making suggestions

Warning: children crossing

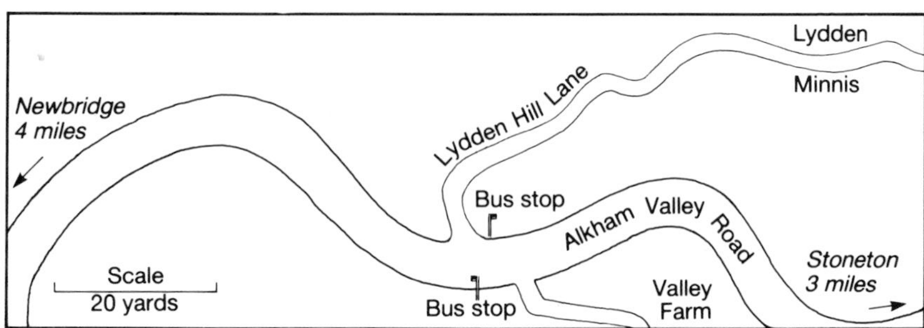

Alarmed by a number of near misses at the junction of Lydden Hill Lane with the Alkham Valley road, some of the residents of the nearby village of Lydden Minnis meet to discuss what should be done.

MRS RALPH I know the problem doesn't just involve the children but their safety has got to be the number-one concern, hasn't it? It's on their way back from school that they're most at risk, so I've got a suggestion: I think we should write to Mr Willgress, the Divisional Education Officer, and ask him to take the matter up for us.

MR DOYLE Sounds a good idea. Would you write the letter?

MRS RALPH Provided we all agree what should go in it.

MRS PIPER Well, I suppose we ought to start by making it clear to him exactly what it is we're worried about. We should explain that the service bus drops the kids off opposite Lydden Hill turn-off and they have to cross over the Alkham Valley road to get to the lane up to the village. Then we've got to make him see what a death-trap that stretch of the valley road is.

MISS IVES Mention there are always one or two parents there to meet the bus – we don't want him to think we aren't doing our bit.

MR DOYLE Right, so the problem really comes down to bad visibility: the bends in the valley road at that point make it impossible to see more than twenty yards or so in either direction. I don't care how careful you are, there's no way you can cross that road safely.

MRS RALPH It's not just the bends though, is it? The high banks on each side of the main road and the overhanging trees and bushes mean that traffic is invisible till it's almost on top of you. All you can do is step off the pavement and pray there's nothing coming.

MISS IVES Except there's no pavement on that side!

MRS RALPH True.

MRS PIPER I'd also mention how much busier the main road is now the new Stoneton bypass feeds into the valley. It never used to be a major route between Stoneton and Newbridge like it is now.

MRS RALPH I think I've jotted down enough on the problem itself. Presumably what we ought to do next is make some suggestions.

MISS IVES Ideally the section of the valley road at the bottom of the hill should be straightened.

MR DOYLE Yes, but we've got to be realistic. Can you see the local authority agreeing to something as expensive as straightening the road? For one thing it would involve demolishing two or three houses in the valley.

MRS PIPER To start with we need warning signs before the bends – 'Children Crossing', that sort of thing.

MRS RALPH And there ought to be a speed restriction on that section of the main road.

MRS PIPER What about one of those crossing attendants or whatever they're called?

MR DOYLE I don't think that's on. Would *you* fancy standing in the middle of that road waving your lollipop at TIRs belting round blind bends? You'd need to be pretty light on your feet!

MISS IVES The obvious thing to do to improve visibility on those bends is to cut back the banking and the trees. That's certainly something we could propose.

MRS RALPH You know what would really solve the problem as far as the schoolchildren are concerned? Having the bus come up into the village itself to collect them and drop them off. It's only a hundred yards off the main road.

MR DOYLE You'd never get a service bus up and down that lane.

MRS RALPH No, I mean if the Education people laid on a minibus. Do they do that?

MISS IVES I'm not sure. But there are fourteen kids who use the service bus so perhaps they'd think it was worthwhile.

MRS PIPER There'd be another advantage if they did that: it would mean the children didn't have to walk up and down the hill. That can be a very dangerous journey in itself, the lane being so winding and narrow.

MRS RALPH All right, I'll suggest that as our main proposal and then list the other things we've said as alternatives. Anything else?

MISS IVES I'd like you to mention there's no lighting at the bottom of the hill. That's really important if the children are going to have to continue using the service bus. In winter it's often dark when they're dropped off; drivers can't see them.

MRS RALPH Right, so lighting at the junction. I can't think of anything more, can you?

MR DOYLE No, I think that's about it. There is one other point though: I think we must be careful the way we put all this. Certainly we've got to show the Education Officer how worried we are and we should be firm, but there'd be no point in giving the impression we're throwing our weight around – not at this stage anyway. Better to put our ideas as suggestions which we want his advice on, and then see whether that approach gets us anywhere.

MRS RALPH Fair enough. I'll put the letter together and then bring it round to the three of you to see what you think.

Writing for a purpose

1 Write Mrs Ralph's letter. You may assume that the sketch map will be sent with the letter if you wish.

Of course, Mr Doyle's remark at the end of the dialogue about the tone of what you write is important: suggestions are not complaints and should not sound as though they are. (See Resource 17, page 111.)

2 Choose some aspect of your school or local community which you consider to be unsatisfactory at the moment and compile a list of ways the situation could be improved. Then write a letter to whomever you think would be an appropriate person to approach, outlining the problem as you see it and describing the measures you believe should be taken. Remember the importance of the tone of your letter if your suggestions are to be received favourably.

You are free to choose any suitable subject, but you might consider dealing with one of the following:

School:	the way assemblies are conducted; the rules that govern fourth year options; break and lunchtime arrangements; the method used to appoint prefects and the powers they are given.
Local community:	the general appearance of the area; recreational facilities for young people; the relations between the police and teenagers; provision for the handicapped.

(See Resource 17, page 111.)

Other writing

Pulling Together

It is surprising what can be done when determined individuals come together and organise themselves to achieve a common goal. Write a short story in which some form of joint action within the family, amongst friends or in the local community produces remarkable results. An account of an actual instance of successful co-operation in which you were involved would be particularly interesting.

22 Publicity for causes

The egg factory

In recent years, egg production in this country has been revolutionised by the introduction of the battery system. Now fewer than 4 per cent of Britain's 45 million laying hens are kept free-range. Instead the practice is to house several thousand birds in one building which is artificially lit, heated and ventilated to encourage maximum laying all the year round and organised to make the most efficient use of labour, space, food and energy. Hens are kept in cages, usually stacked in tiers and stepped so that droppings fall through the wire floors into a pit beneath – a typical arrangement is shown in the diagram. A cage 525 mm (20.7 in) wide, 450 mm (17.7 in) deep and 450 mm (17.7 in) high would normally house four or five birds for over a year. In the most modern units, feeding, watering and egg collection are all fully automatic.

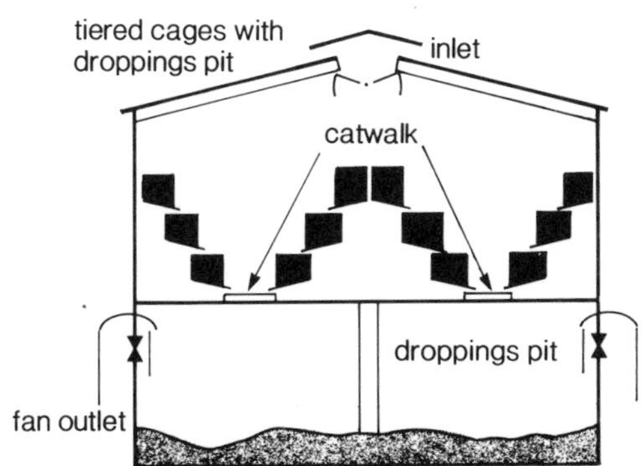

THE CASE FOR CAGES

The cage system has been developed over fifty years of practical use to overcome the disadvantages of other systems, including free-range flocks.

If hens are kept in flocks, especially out of doors, they are much more prone to disease from parasites and are very vulnerable to attack from predators, foxes and mink in particular. Moreover, in flocks hens develop what is called a 'peck order', a ranking amongst the birds in which those lower down the order are attacked by their 'seniors' and often find it very difficult to secure enough food for themselves; cannibalism is by no means rare. As a result it is a common practice to remove part of the hens' beaks so that they can inflict less injury. Hens kept in cages do not develop these 'vices' and debeaking is therefore normally unnecessary. Each bird has free access to food and water at all times and consequently a better opportunity of getting its share without undue competition from its neighbours.

A further, very real danger associated with keeping hens in flocks is a tendency they have to become 'hysterical': a sudden noise or other disturbance will send them crowding into a corner, desperately scrambling over each other, causing those at the bottom of the pile to suffocate. This simply cannot happen in cages in which there are only four or five birds.

Free-range hens can suffer stress from extremes of temperature and the varying day-lengths. A return to this system would mean, in addition to discomfort for the birds, a very uneven supply of eggs – a glut in the spring and shortage in winter – and, as a result, big seasonal fluctuations in the price of eggs in the shops. In the battery system, artificial lighting ensures that the lengths of day and night are constant throughout the year and the units are kept at an even 60° to 70°F, the temperature at which hens are happiest, coming as they do from jungle ancestors.

In all these ways, the battery system creates an environment which suits the birds and protects their well-being. It has additional benefits for the egg-consumer, in other words, for most members of the public.

The regularity of supply has already been mentioned. Also it is rare now to see a dirty egg on the shop counter, thanks to the fact that battery cages keep eggs clear of manure; and because they are easy to see and collect, the bad egg is a rarity too.

However, the chief benefit to the consumer lies in the price of eggs. The cost of keeping hens on free range is just about double that of keeping them in batteries. If all eggs sold in this country were free-range, they would be beyond the pocket of many consumers; lower income families and old people would be particularly hard hit since they rely on eggs as a major source of protein. In fact, egg prices have fallen by nearly 50 per cent since the early 1960s. This is mainly due to the efficiency of the battery cage system which has produced ample supplies of high quality eggs. Abolition of the battery cage would set the industry, and the consumer, back a full twenty years.

NATIONAL FARMERS' UNION
The Case for Cages, adapted leaflet

Song of the Battery Hen

We can't grumble about accommodation:
we have a new concrete floor that's
always dry, four walls that are
painted white, and a sheet-iron roof
the rain drums on. A fan blows warm air
beneath our feet to disperse the smell
of chicken-shit and, on dull days,
fluorescent lighting sees us.

You can tell me: if you come by
the North door, I am in the twelfth pen
on the left-hand side of the third row
from the floor; and in that pen
I am usually the middle one of three.
But, even without directions, you'd
discover me. I have the same orange-
red comb, yellow beak and auburn
feathers, but as the door opens and you
hear above the electric fan a kind of
one-word wail, I am the one
who sounds loudest in my head.

Listen. Outside this house there's an
orchard with small moss-green apple
trees; beyond that, two fields of
cabbages; then, on the far side of
the road, a broiler house. Listen:
one cockerel grows out of there, as
tall and proud as the first hour of sun.
Sometimes I stop calling with the others
to listen, and wonder if he hears me.
The next time you come here, look for me.
Notice the way I sound inside my head.
God made us all quite differently,
and blessed us with this expensive home.

EDWIN BROCK

Writing for a purpose

1 You will probably have been given the chance to discuss the material above and to make up your mind on the very controversial matter of battery egg production. Groups who feel strongly on such important issues will often try to promote their

views through newspaper advertisements and leaflets they distribute to the public. Of course, charities use the same means to win support for their work.

Prepare a leaflet or advertisement in which you attack or defend the battery system and try to persuade others to share your point of view. Obviously your aim must be to make the maximum impact on the reader, so before you begin, you should examine examples of such material and consider the methods they use to get their message across. A mere emotional appeal is not enough: only a well-argued case based on facts deserves to be taken seriously. (See Resource 19, pages 114 and 115.)

2 Produce a leaflet or advertisement of the kind described in Exercise 1 in which you try to win support for one of the following:
  a the work of a pressure group or charity of which you approve – for example, Amnesty International, the National Anti-Vivisection Society, Help the Aged, the Royal National Lifeboat Institution;
  b your views on an issue you feel is important – for example, capital punishment, abortion, nuclear disarmament, seal culls, youth unemployment.

(See Resource 19, pages 114 and 115.)

Other writing

Worlds Apart

You will have read poems, short stories or novels in which the characters are animals. If the creatures are simply made to think, feel and behave as we would in their situation, the result can be childishly unconvincing; the most successful work of this kind attempts to imagine what it is really like to be an animal, as Edwin Brock does so well in the poem on page 79. Bearing this in mind, write a story or poem in which the narrator is an animal and you give an account of a particular episode – a fox hunt, for example – or of the more ordinary experiences of a pet perhaps, or an animal exhibited in a zoo or circus.

23 Letters to The Editor

Teenage attitudes

These findings, published in 1983, are based on interviews with 635 young people aged fourteen to nineteen and more or less representative of British teenagers:

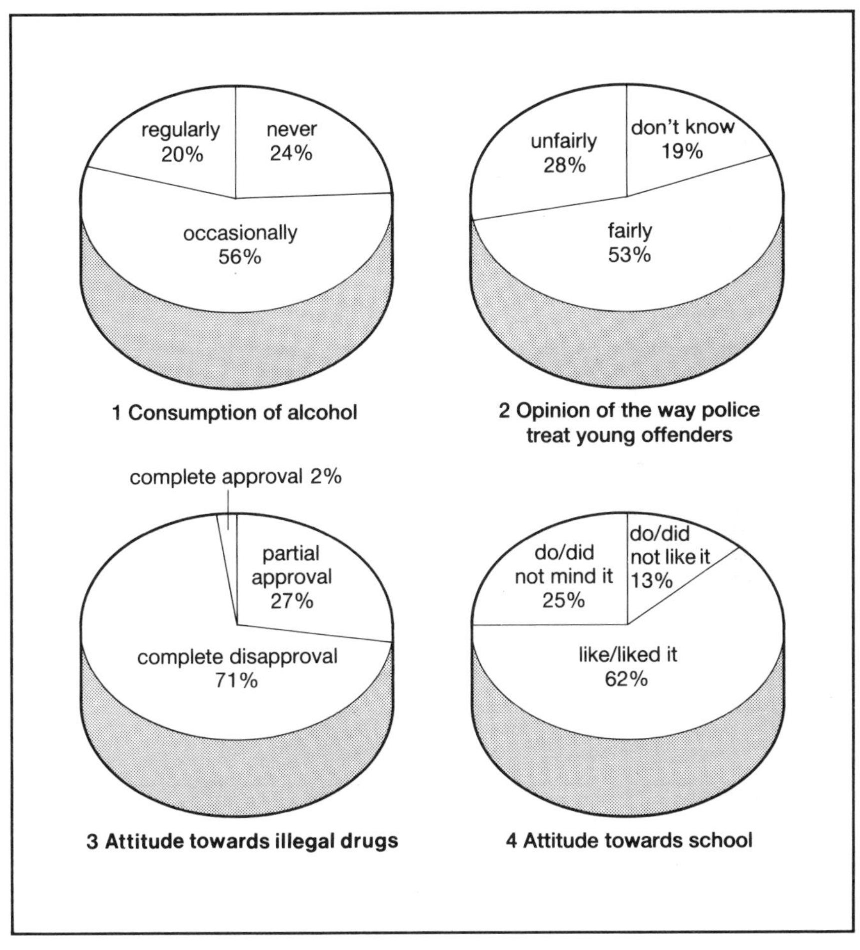

1 Consumption of alcohol

2 Opinion of the way police treat young offenders

3 Attitude towards illegal drugs

4 Attitude towards school

5 Social concerns
People ought to do what they can to help:
71%
the elderly
58%
conserve the countryside
66%
the handicapped
61%
campaign for jobs
70%
make towns better to live in
49%
the Third World

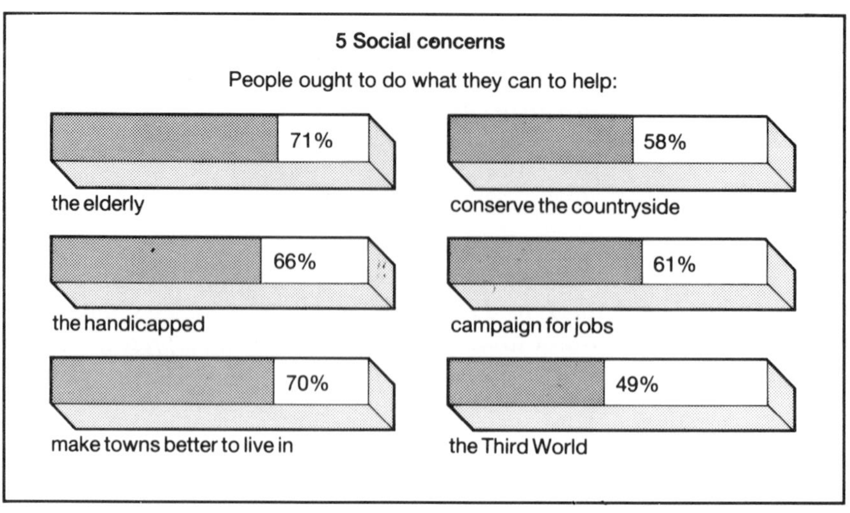

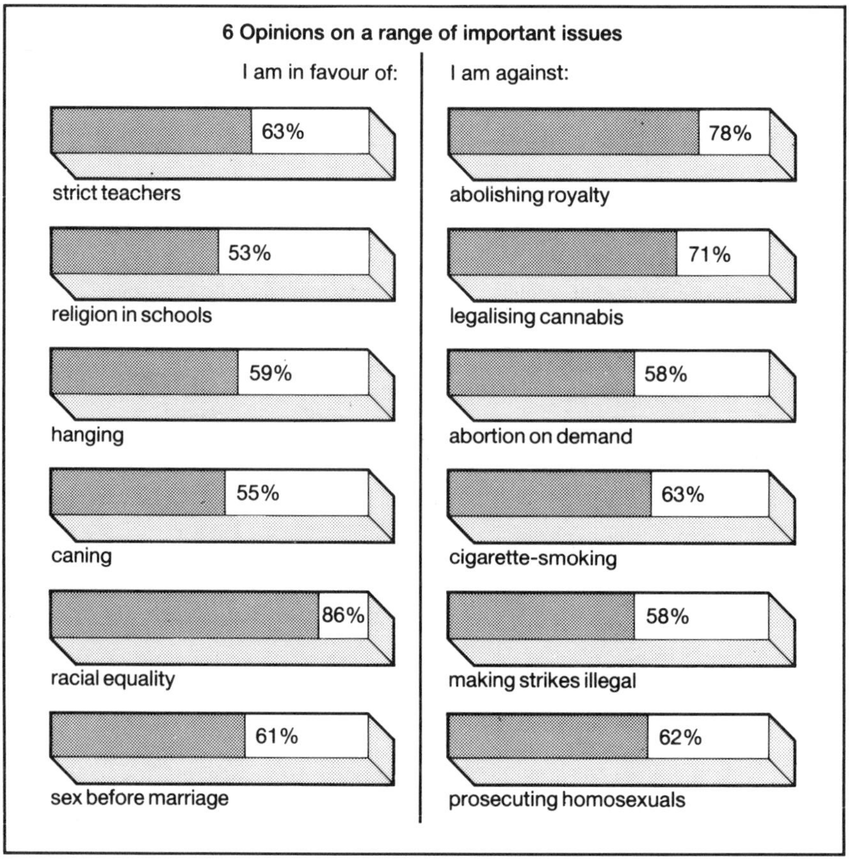

6 Opinions on a range of important issues
I am in favour of:
I am against:
63%
strict teachers
78%
abolishing royalty
53%
religion in schools
71%
legalising cannabis
59%
hanging
58%
abortion on demand
55%
caning
63%
cigarette-smoking
86%
racial equality
58%
making strikes illegal
61%
sex before marriage
62%
prosecuting homosexuals

Writing for a purpose

1 This letter appears in a newspaper:

> Sir, I know I speak for the majority of your older readers when I say I despair of modern youth – this appallingly irresponsible generation who have turned their backs on traditional ideas of right and wrong and apparently believe 'anything goes'.
>
> The root cause of this sorry state of affairs lies in their complete rejection of authority. They have no time for parents, school, the police or indeed anything or anyone representing discipline and decent values. We are all too aware of the evil habits and general immorality this has led them to.
>
> In my experience, they are a selfish, discontented shower who could not care less about other people and the society in which they live.
>
> Compulsory national service, to my mind, is what these youngsters of ours need. A spell in the armed forces certainly did not do their fathers any harm!
>
> B J Drayton (Brigadier, retired)
> Leamington Spa

Fortunately, the survey suggests the Brigadier's impression of young people is mistaken. Write a letter for publication in the same newspaper, taking issue with his attack on your generation and pointing out clearly where his allegations are wrong. Of course, you will be making use of the facts revealed by the survey, but do not overburden your letter with a welter of percentages. Bear in mind that the Editor is unlikely to publish your letter if it is longer than 250 words.

2 Write to a newspaper, replying to a letter it has published which expresses one of the following opinions:

a modern youngsters are mindless slaves to fashion in music and clothes; they haven't got the sense to realise what rubbish they're being conned with;

b all this fuss about women's rights is just the ravings of hysterical spinsters who want to justify their own inadequacies;

c if it is true there is a 'generation gap' between young people and their parents, the fault nearly always lies with the former;

d most people who are unemployed must like it that way: there's always work for those determined enough to find it in their home area or elsewhere in the country;

e the lack of interest taken by British teenagers in the politics of their country shows how little they deserve the privilege of living in a democracy.

It is not enough, of course, simply to deny the truth of the opinion; you must argue your case carefully, supporting it with hard facts where necessary. Your letter should be no longer than 250 words.

Other writing

Cause for Concern
Look again at Table 5 on page 82 and choose one of the concerns listed there which you agree ought to be taken seriously. Then write an essay in which you explain why you think the present situation needs attention and consider practical ways the community as a whole and individual young people in particular could do something to improve matters.

The Generation Gap
Members of different age groups so often seem to view each other with suspicion and a failure of understanding and sympathy. Make this so-called generation gap the theme of a short story or poem.

24 Discussion and minutes of meetings

An exchange of views

Schools often have advisory councils composed of representatives of the staff and pupils who meet to discuss matters of concern. These are the minutes of such a meeting:

Minutes of a meeting of the School Council held on 16th September 19- at 4 00 p.m.

Absences: Apologies had been received from Mr H Williams and Geoffrey Isles (third year) who were unable to attend.

Previous minutes: These were read by the Secretary and approved as an accurate record.

Matters arising from previous minutes

a Mr Sharp informed the meeting that the cold drinks machine had now been ordered and would be installed during the half-term holiday.

b Jane Grieves (fourth year) wondered why the roller towels in the girls' cloakroom were still not being changed often enough. Mr Norton said he would raise the matter again with the caretaker.

Main agenda

a Homework Gloria Hyde (third year) was concerned about the amount of homework set in the school. She could not see that so much was necessary and thought it restricted pupils' social life unduly and stopped them pursuing their own interests. Mrs Whiteman argued that homework increased self-discipline and developed a capacity for independent learning. However, several student members considered that homework unfairly penalised certain pupils whose home backgrounds discouraged private study. Mr Norton thought that homework helped consolidate classroom learning and said he would be reluctant to reduce the amount given.

b Corporal punishment Trevor Pryor (sixth form) argued that corporal punishment brutalised staff and pupils alike, was not effective anyway and therefore ought to be abolished. Mr Norton generally agreed and said that during his five years as headmaster no-one had been caned. Student members insisted that individual teachers resorted to physical punishment quite regularly. Mrs Collins thought mild correction of the sort under discussion could have beneficial effects. The majority of the Council could not agree and Mr Norton promised the question would be discussed at the next staff meeting.

Any other business

Lisa James (second year) asked if the hall could be swept more often since juniors had to sit on the floor during assemblies. Mr Norton said the problem had resulted from the cut in the number of school cleaners but agreed to see what could be done.

The next meeting having been fixed for 7th October 19- and there being no other business, the meeting closed at 5.15 p.m.

Brian Thorpe.

Brian Thorpe Secretary

Writing for a purpose

1 Minutes provide a most useful record of discussions and decisions. However, they are a very formal, much condensed version of what actually took place and they usually give little sense of the reality of a group of individuals reacting to each other's arguments and struggling to make their views convincing. Discussions are often intense and dramatic, but this will not normally be obvious from the minutes.

Choose one of the main items on the agenda of the School Council meeting – homework or corporal punishment – and re-create the original discussion, using the dialogue form. Rather than producing a series of unrelated speeches, you should aim to capture the give and take of a real exchange of arguments and opinions. You are free to introduce characters not named in the minutes.

2 Imagine a meeting the agenda of which has only one main item. The meeting might be called, for example, by one of the following:

a a school council to discuss whether or not uniform should be abolished;

b the committee of a youth club to decide what can be done to attract more members;

c a residents' group concerned about vandalism on their estate and how it can be controlled.

Using the dialogue form, present the discussion of the topic which took place. Make the participants react in a realistic but reasonable way to each other's arguments and suggestions.

Then write the minutes of the meeting you have just invented. In addition to the main discussion, record less important items on the agenda like 'Any other business' so that you produce a complete set of minutes.

Other writing

The Right to Decide?

Schools are sometimes criticised as very undemocratic institutions from your point of view; it is suggested that pupils are entitled to a far greater say in what happens in their schools – how and what they are taught, for example, and what rules, if any, there should be. What are your own thoughts on the question? Do not feel you have to argue for or against greater pupil democracy; it is better perhaps to aim at a balanced discussion in which you consider what is to be said on both sides.

25 Articles reporting surveys

Teenage lives

These are further findings from the survey of young people's opinions and lives which was used in unit 23:

INCOME
14- to 16-year-olds

1. Disposable income*		2. Sources of income	
I have . . . to spend a week.	%	I get money from . . .	%
less than £2	44	my parents.	84
£2 – £4.99	39	my relatives.	23
£5 – £9.99	13	a part-time job.	28
£10 – £15	3	doing odd jobs.	20
more than £15	1		

3. Savings		4. Attitude towards income	
I . . . save money.	%	I consider my income . . .	%
never	20	enough for someone my age.	57
regularly	29	not enough but I manage.	38
occasionally	51	nowhere near enough.	5

* The survey was conducted in 1981; presumably young people generally have rather more money to spend today.

EXPENDITURE
14- to 19-year-olds

5. Items of expenditure

I spend money on:	Male %	Female %	I spend money on:	Male %	Female %
Clothes	43	70	Alcohol	24	12
Shoes	17	28	Records/tapes	50	32
Toiletries	6	32	Discos/clubs	37	42
Make-up	1	35	Comics/magazines	17	24
Chips/hamburgers	36	26	Books	13	18
Crisps/sweets	29	33	Cigarettes	20	12
Soft drinks	11	10	Sports	27	22

LEISURE
14- to 19-year-olds

6. Leisure activities			7. Sporting activities		
I regularly . . .	Male %	Female %	I regularly participate in . . .	Male %	Female %
listen to music. } at home	55	60	some sport.	75	53
watch TV. } at home	50	55	football.	27	1
read books/magazines. } at home	27	47	cricket.	9	1
go out with friends.	49	44	athletics.	12	6
go out with opposite sex.	26	28	swimming.	16	12
go to discos.	20	24	badminton.	7	8
go to pubs.	23	19	netball.	0	12
go to the cinema.	7	2	pool.	24	3
go to the sports centre.	33	14	table tennis.	16	4
go to the youth club.	16	13	martial arts.	14	1

HOME AND PARENTS
14- to 19-year-olds

8. Help at home			9. Attitudes of parents		
I regularly . . .	Male %	Female %	My parents . . .	Male %	Female %
make my own bed.	47	77	insist on knowing where I'm going.	60	82
wash up.	22	57	are strict about time.	29	36
help clean the house.	13	42	worry about me getting into fights.	42	24
get the shopping.	21	30	worry about boy/girl trouble.	20	29
cook a meal.	7	27	disapprove of most of my leisure activities.	20	14
look after the animals.	15	24			
do some gardening.	9	4			
clean the car.	10	5			

Writing for a purpose

1 When national surveys of this kind appear, it is usual for newspapers to report their findings. Imagine that this particular survey – which was entitled *Young People in the Eighties* and was conducted for the Government – has just been published, and write a newspaper article summarising what it reveals about the lives of teenagers.

The tables contain a great deal of interesting information. Obviously you cannot cover it all, so select a few of what you consider the most noteworthy findings and build your article around those. If you are to produce something readable, you must avoid overwhelming your reader with a long list of percentages. You may assume that the tables you decide to use will be printed with your article; therefore your task is to interpret and comment on what they reveal, not necessarily to quote them in detail. (See Resource 18, page 112 and 113.)

2 Conduct your own survey into some area of young people's lives or opinions by compiling a number of questions which you will ask members of your class. Record their answers and then express your findings as percentages in a table like those on pages 87 and 88. You might choose one of the following topics:

a How large a part music/reading/television plays in their lives and what their preferences are.

b How they feel about certain aspects of school life. Are there any rules they object to? Which subjects do they like/dislike the most? Are there subjects they would like to see added to the timetable? How well do they consider staff and pupils get on together? And so forth.

c What their views are on the Royal Family/the Church/football hooliganism/their parents' generation.

d How they see their futures in terms of further education, employment, marriage and so on.

When you have done this, write an article that could accompany the results of your survey if they were to appear in the school magazine. What is required here is explained in Exercise 1. (See Resource 18, page 112 and 113.)

Other writing

They're not like us

Tables 5–9 seem to indicate differences between the attitudes and interests of boys and those of girls. Of course, such differences are supposed to run deep. Girls, we are told, tend to be, for example, more emotional, inconsistent and caring; whereas the average boy is more aggressive, competitive and logical.

Write an essay in which you discuss the following questions and/or any other aspects of the subject which interest you:

What would be a fuller description of the supposed differences in personality between the sexes? In your experience, is there any truth in these generalisations? If differences do exist, are they inbred or due to some other cause? If they do not really exist, why do so many of us seem to imagine they do?

Resource File

1 A factual account

Heavy winds during the night of 22nd March 1986 dislodged a number of roof-tiles, letting the rain into the attic. The next morning, unable to find a builder prepared to do the repair at short notice, I felt I must tackle the job myself. Having secured the base of a twenty-foot ladder to a stake driven into my lawn, I climbed onto the roof and was engaged in replacing the tiles when my exertions on the ladder caused it to begin to move. It slid sideways off the roof and I managed to prevent myself falling with it only by clinging to the chimney-stack.

My four-year-old daughter had witnessed the incident but I could not get her to grasp the seriousness of the situation or fetch help. Since shouting for several minutes failed to attract anyone else's attention, I decided I must make some attempt to get back to the ground unaided. I worked my way slowly across the roof to the drainpipe at the corner of the house and, with the utmost caution, started to descend.

Unfortunately the bolts anchoring the drainpipe to the brickwork were unable to bear my weight and the pipe came away from the wall, swinging me out over the greenhouse before collapsing and dropping me through the glass roof. I sustained deep cuts to my legs, hands and chin from the broken glass, mild concussion when the drainpipe struck my head and a fractured left ankle.

At this point my daughter seems to have realised that I was not merely clowning and fetched my wife; an ambulance was summoned. I was admitted to Bromley General Hospital, discharged two days later and was not well enough to return to work until 9th April 1986.

2 Advice leaflets

The heavy cost of motoring

Ten easy ways to make a little go a long way

1 See that your car is properly tuned and serviced.

2 Make sure your tyres are at the right pressure.

3 Always use the recommended grade of petrol.

4 Push in the choke as soon as the car will run smoothly without it.

5 Try to anticipate what other drivers are going to do, so that you can ...

6 Avoid heavy braking. This is the biggest fuel waster.

7 Accelerate smoothly.

8 Choose a sensible cruising speed. At 70mph you can be using over a third more petrol than at 50.

9 Don't carry unnecessary weight in your car. It uses extra fuel, especially when you accelerate or climb hills.

10 Roof racks increase wind resistance. If you have one, take it off when you are not using it.

Keep a check on your mpg. See how you can save petrol. And money.

If you would like more information about petrol saving, write to 'Fuel Saving', Department of Transport, Publicity Stores, Building No. 3, Victoria Road, South Ruislip, Middx. HA4 ON2.

Prepared by the Department of Transport and the Central Office of Information. 1982

Printed in England for Her Majesty's Stationery Office by Maybank Press Ltd. Dd. 8299180 Pro. 18625

WINNING THE VOTE
A Guide to Writing Debate Speeches

- If there are two of you to speak on the one side, do not repeat the same arguments. Divide them between you before you begin to write your speech.
- You may think there is something to be said on both sides of the question. For the purposes of the debate, however, do not concede anything to your opponent.
- When preparing your speech, never forget it is aimed at *listeners* not readers. Subtle spoken arguments are not easy to follow, so your points must be made simply and strongly. Similarly, very general statements often make little impact on a listener; they need to be supported by well-chosen examples that make your meaning clear and fix it in the audience's mind.
- The relevance of your remarks should always be obvious. The topic being debated should be kept before the listener and everything you have to say clearly related to it.
- An audience appreciates and responds to a lively, entertaining speaker. You must try to express yourself in a striking way and, if possible and appropriate, with humour.
- Make some attempt to involve your listeners. Address yourself directly to them so that each of your hearers feels you are speaking to him or her individually: 'How would you like it if . . .?' 'What I want you to consider is . . .'.
- Never just make your last point and then sit down. End with a brief summing-up of your case and a final appeal for the audience's support.
- If your opponent is speaking first, listen carefully to what he or she has to say and try to be flexible enough to relate your own arguments to the ones your opponent has made.
- When you deliver your speech, never mumble, gabble or keep your eyes riveted to your notes. It is a confident, relaxed and, of course, a clearly audible style of delivery that most impresses an audience.
- Avoid simply reading your speech. Speaking from a set of notes is much more convincing, even though you may have written your speech in full and have merely learnt it more or less by heart.

3 Description of a 'machine'

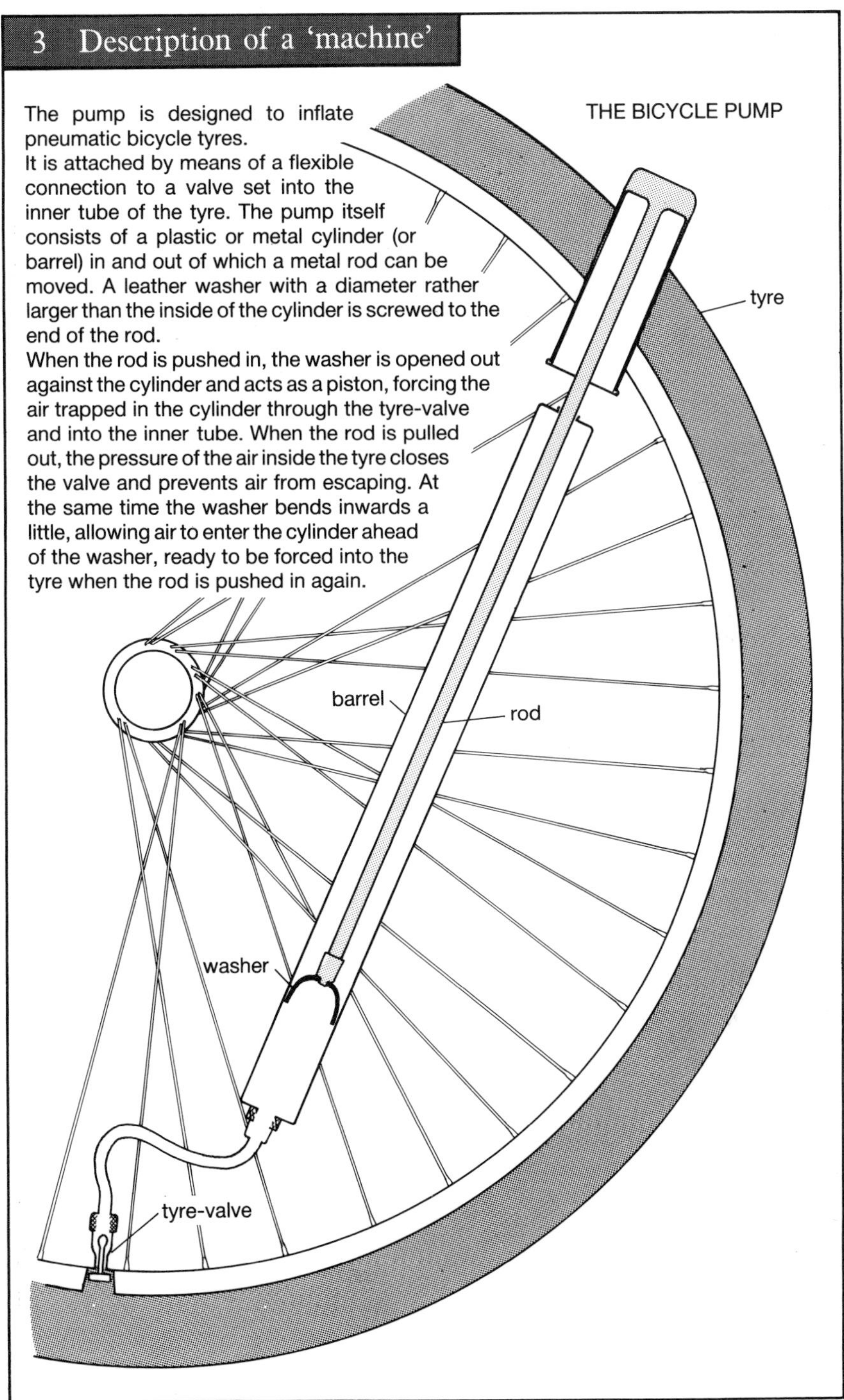

The pump is designed to inflate pneumatic bicycle tyres.
It is attached by means of a flexible connection to a valve set into the inner tube of the tyre. The pump itself consists of a plastic or metal cylinder (or barrel) in and out of which a metal rod can be moved. A leather washer with a diameter rather larger than the inside of the cylinder is screwed to the end of the rod.
When the rod is pushed in, the washer is opened out against the cylinder and acts as a piston, forcing the air trapped in the cylinder through the tyre-valve and into the inner tube. When the rod is pulled out, the pressure of the air inside the tyre closes the valve and prevents air from escaping. At the same time the washer bends inwards a little, allowing air to enter the cylinder ahead of the washer, ready to be forced into the tyre when the rod is pushed in again.

4 Instructions

EMERGENCY AND: WHAT TO DO IF A PERSON STOPS BREATHING

If a casualty's breathing does not start again within 3 minutes and so restore oxygen to the brain, he or she will die. So you must act quickly. Lay the person gently on his or her back and then:

1 Check that there is nothing in the mouth that is stopping his or her breathing. If there is, you will probably be able to remove it with a finger, but be careful you do not simply push the obstruction further down the throat.
2 If you can see no obstruction or if, after removing it, breathing does not start, the tongue may have fallen back and be blocking the airway. Place one hand on the forehead, the other under the neck and tilt the head back. Opening the air passage like this may be enough, but if breathing does not resume, you must try mouth-to-mouth ventilation:
3 Loosen any tight clothing round the neck.
4 Take a deep breath, pinch the person's nostrils together and put your lips round his mouth. In the case of children, their small faces might mean that your mouth has to cover their noses as well.
5 Looking along the chest, blow until you see the chest rise. With children you would obviously need to blow less air into the lungs.
6 Move your mouth away, finish breathing out and watch for the chest to fall.
7 Then take in fresh air and repeat the process. Give the first 4 breaths quickly, then continue at the normal rate (15 or 16 breaths a minute).
8 You must keep on breathing for the person until:
a he or she starts breathing for himself/herself,
b someone takes over from you, or
c qualified help arrives.
Do not give up: the person may recover even after needing a long session of mouth-to-mouth ventilation.
9 If the casualty resumes breathing, he or she should be moved to the recovery position.

5 Directions

. . . Immediately opposite the Royal George, a stile marks the start of a section of the North Downs Way which leads to the beautiful little village of Pentworth, a mile distant. On your right, fifty yards or so along the footpath, the granite slab of the Bleriot monument indicates the spot where the famous French aviator's first cross-Channel flight ended in July 1909. Shortly after the monument, the path crosses Blackwater Stream by means of a rickety wooden bridge – you will need to take care here – and then divides. You should take the left fork which skirts the base of Sugarloaf Hill and joins Pentworth Lane a few yards north of Blackwater Mill. Notice, just before you enter the lane, a few scattered limestone blocks on your right – all that remains of Pentworth Abbey, founded in 1428 and finally abandoned in the middle of the last century. Blackwater Mill itself is well worth a visit; it has recently been restored and is now in full working order . . .

6 A personal report

COPPER CABLE AND WIRE COMPANY LIMITED
ANNUAL JUNIOR STAFF ASSESSMENT YEAR: 1985/6

Employee: MISS ROBERTA GOVONS *Age:* 20

Position: Assistant Secretary

Number of years with the company: 2 years

Number of years in present position: 2 years

1. *Punctuality and attendance:* Very good

2. *Attitude towards work:* Miss Govons seems to enjoy her work and is most conscientious: she takes a pride in whatever she does and is prepared to go to great trouble to get things right.

3. *Quality of work:* Excellent: she works fast but very accurately. Her attention to detail and sense of layout are impressive, and she is rarely required to repeat a piece of work.

4. *Initiative:* She is happy working independently of supervision and can be relied on to apply sound common sense to any problems she might meet.

5. *Attitude towards senior staff:* She does tend to be rather sensitive to criticism and her defensiveness means it is not always easy to offer her guidance. As she gains in confidence and becomes surer of her position in the company the problem should ease.

6. *Suitability for promotion:* I recommend promotion to full secretary in the near future. The quality of her work certainly merits it and our recognition of her worth may well help her overcome the tendency mentioned in 5.

Date: 4th August 1986 J. Sprigett

Chief Clerk

7 Live radio commentary

27th August 1944: General de Gaulle enters liberated Paris

'Immediately behind me through the great doors of this thirteenth-century cathedral (of Notre Dame) I can see, in this dim half-light, a mass of faces turned towards the door, waiting for the arrival of General de Gaulle, and when the General arrives, this huge concourse of people both inside and outside the cathedral, they'll be joining in a celebration of the solemn *Te Deum* in the mother church of France.

'In front of me are lined up the men and women of the French Resistance Movement; they're a variegated set of boys and girls – some of the men are dressed in dungarees, overalls, some look rather smart, the bank-clerk type, some are in very shabby suits but they've all got their red, white and blue armlets with the blue Cross of Lorraine, and they're all armed, they've got their rifles slung over their shoulders and their bandoliers strapped round their waist. And now here comes General de Gaulle. The General's now turned to face the square, and this huge crowd of Parisians (*machine-gun fire*). He's being presented to people (*machine-gun fire*). He's being received (*shouts of crowd – shots*) even while the General is marching (*sudden sharp outburst of continued fire*) – even while the General is marching into the cathedral …… *Break on record.*

'Well, that was one of the most dramatic scenes I've ever seen. Just as General de Gaulle was about to enter the Cathedral of Notre Dame, firing started all over the place. He walked straight ahead in what appeared to me to be a hail of fire from somewhere inside the cathedral – somewhere from the galleries up near the vaulted roof. But he went straight ahead without hesitation, his shoulders flung back, and walked right down the central aisle, even while bullets were pouring around him. It was the most extraordinary example of courage that I've ever seen.'

ROBERT REID

20th September 1944: supplies are dropped to Allied troops surrounded at Arnhem

'Just a few minutes ago the fighter cover showed up and right behind them came those lovely supply planes which you can hear up above us now. Yesterday and this morning our supplies came and were dropped in the wrong place. The enemy got them, but now these planes have come over and they've dropped them right dead over us.

'Everybody is cheering and clapping and they just can't give vent to their feelings about what a wonderful sight this is. All those bundles and parachuted packages and ammunition are coming down here all around us, through the trees, bouncing on the ground, the men are running to get them, and you have no idea what this means to us to see this ammunition and this food coming down where the men can get it. They're such fighters, if they can only get the stuff to fight with. You can hear the flak that those planes are flying through, it's absolutely like . . . (*noise of flak*) . . . hail up there. The enemy guns all around us are simply hammering at those planes, but so far I haven't seen anything, I haven't seen any of them hit, but bundles are coming down, the parachutes are coming down . . . (*noise of planes and flak*).'

STANLEY MAXTED

26th April 1945: the German city of Bremen is captured

'I am in the centre of the city of Bremen, if you can call this chaotic rubbish-heap in which our bulldozers are working as I speak, their men with handkerchiefs round their throats to avoid the flying dust, if you can call this rubbish-heap a city any more. There are walls standing, there are factory chimneys here and there, but there's no shape and no order and certainly no hope for this shell of a city that was once called Bremen. It's the sheer size of the smashed area that overwhelms you. These endless vistas down small streets to the houses leaning at drunken angles and this inhuman landscape of great blocks of flats with their sides ripped open, and the intimate household goods just blown out into the bomb craters. Well, I expected it when we came in, but still it's the scale that counts.

WYNFORD VAUGHAN-THOMAS

8 Magazine advice

Friendly quarrels

I am a girl of 12, and my friend Sharon and I are the best of pals and have been going round with each other for about a year. There is one problem, though. We always fall out over the stupidest things. Have you any advice how to stop this?

Amanda
Cheshire

The trouble between you and your friend is that you are becoming bored with each other. It is wonderful to have a close friendship, but never advisable to keep it exclusive. The tiffs you have are perfectly natural among young girls, and if I were you I would include more friends in your circle next term, so you can all swap ideas and chat. You and Sharon could also choose a silly phrase like 'fish and chips' or 'cat and dog'. Agree that whenever an argument starts one of you will say it. This should make you giggle, shut up and then change the subject. Above all, don't lose your sense of fun. All relationships need this and perhaps the problem is that your friendship has lost this quality.

Slowly does it

I left school recently and, fortunately, found a job immediately in a company the name of which starts with a 'G'. Ever since I can remember, I have had a speech difficulty and I stutter now and again, especially with words beginning with 'G', 'W' and 'B'. As you can guess, I have trouble saying the name of my company. I am not a shy person and consider myself to be very confident, but this problem is now making me rather anxious.

Judy
Essex

It would happen, wouldn't it? Please try not to worry – I'm sure you know that to tighten up makes matters worse. Ron Turrell, secretary of the Association for Stammerers, says a speech therapist could certainly help you. Learning to relax is also helpful and, above all, take your time and don't try to talk too fast. The latest aid for people who stutter is a tiny electronic gadget that monitors their speech rate and gives a warning signal when its wearer starts to speed up. Write to the Association of Stammerers, The Finsbury Centre, Pine Street, London EC1R 0JH, for pamphlets and a list of speech therapists, plus the addresses of 70–80 self-help groups across the country. If anyone has a friend who stutters, they should be patient and never attempt to finish off their sentences for them.

Suspect action

I am 14 and have started to avoid certain shops because of the attitude of the shopkeepers and their assistants. They are so suspicious, following me around; if I pause to look at something, they come and rearrange nearby shelves. I don't object to a bit of discreet 'watching' and I sympathise with the fact that they lose items, but I am starting to feel quite guilty, ill at ease and self-conscious. Surely they could rearrange goods so as not to create such an easy target for shoplifters.

Katherine
Devon

If shopkeepers could make their goods thief-proof, I assure you they would. It's not much fun keeping an eye on stock. Try to let these 'minders' know that you understand their anxiety by asking to be shown, or for permission to see, goods that interest you. Or carry the garment towards the assistant and make some comment about it. I am sure they hate playing detective as much as you dislike being made to feel uncomfortable. But, in this case, my sympathies are mainly with the assistants.

T V TIMES

9 Formal letter concerning arrangements

Royal
Elizabethan Theatre
The Embankment
London WC4H 7YG
Telephone: (01) 494 63444

Our reference:
Your reference:

4th June 19–

Mr R.K. Benchley,
Elm Vale Community School,
Halifax HF28 7DK.

Dear Sir,

Thank you for your letter of 19th May. I hope the following information will answer your enquiries.

Unfortunately we are not able to offer reduced rates to school parties attending regular performances: the advertised ticket prices apply. However, where large parties are concerned, complimentary tickets are available to accompanying members of staff. These are provided on the basis of one free ticket for every twenty-five purchased. In the case of your own visit, therefore, since you indicate that you will be bringing sixty-two pupils, you are entitled to tickets for yourself and a colleague free of charge.

We do organise tours of the theatre complex and the exhibition hall for school parties. These begin at 5.45 p.m. and, before matinee performances on Wednesdays and Saturdays, at 12.30 p.m. There is no charge for this service but we do need tour bookings to be made at least two weeks in advance.

Please write to me again if there is any further information you require or I can help in any other way.

Yours faithfully,

Samantha Dee

Education Department

10 A newspaper article

Two injured in window dive horror

CROWDS of Saturday afternoon shoppers froze in horror as two men plunged through a plate glass window in Maidstone town centre.

by LEE BARNDEN

One man sustained horrific head injuries and a woman bystander was seen to faint.

The men had been arguing about a former girlfriend and started pushing each other as crowds stood back.

Then with a tremendous bang the large plate glass window at Bowketts former bakery shop, in Week Street smashed, sending large splinters of glass flying across the road.

Both men remained on their feet although one was bleeding profusely.

One man drove himself to hospital and the other was taken by ambulance.

A police spokesman said: "One of them had horrific injuries to his head and back. The cuts went through to the bone. He needed a lot of stitches."

Both men were released from hospital — the more seriously hurt being kept in overnight.

No charges have been preferred but both men may be summonsed for threatening behaviour.

The police spokesman said: "Both men made up afterwards and, after it was pointed out to them, appreciated how stupid their behaviour was."

Shopper Margaret Vaughan of Gillingham said: "People were flabbergasted by what was happening. There was so much glass about, it crunched underfoot.

"People were concerned about their children and one lady fainted. It was lucky no-one else was hurt.

"Blood was pumping out of one man's head wounds and it amazed me that he was still standing up."

KENT MESSENGER *4th October 1985*

11 A situation report in letter form

J H Begshaw Ltd

Landscape Gardeners
12 East Street
Denley DN4 7YH
Telephone: (0901) 48562

Our reference: GA/SM-2
Your reference:

13th May 19-

Mr. H. Marks,
Yew Tree Cottage,
Medchurch Lane,
Denley.

Dear Sir,

Yew Tree Cottage

In accordance with your instructions we have now inspected the grounds of the above property and are pleased to submit our observations and recommendations. We are enclosing an estimate for the work we consider necessary and we would, of course, be happy to undertake the improvements if instructed to do so.

Fencing This is generally sound though in need of treatment with wood preservative. A ten-foot section of the fence to the rear of the property is, however, badly rotted and requires replacing.

The Drive The asphalt has broken up in several places and is now unsightly. The drive needs complete resurfacing.

Flower-beds Generally the beds are sparse and unattractive, and require restocking with a more imaginative, colourful selection of plants. The rose-bed adjoining the north-facing wall of the property is not well situated: due to the poor sunlight the roses are weakly and constitute a poor display. They need to be replaced with bedding plants more suited to the conditions.

Trees Nearly all the trees on the property badly need drastic pruning since at present they are a hazard in high winds. The elm in the south-east corner is dead; it should be felled and its roots removed.

Should there be any matters you would like to discuss further, we hope you will not hesitate to get in touch with us.

Yours faithfully,

G. Ashcroft
Manager

Enc.

Directors: L Jones A Healy T Jackson Registered office: as above Registered number: 294331 England

12 A job application

180 Fulford Road,
Fenton FN7 8YG.

Mr. R. Caulfield,
Image Studios,
6, The Precinct,
Fenton.

3rd April, 19–

Dear Mr. Caulfield,

I would like to apply for the position of general assistant which was advertised in this week's 'Fenton Post'.

I am in the fifth year at St. Mark's Secondary School and shall be leaving this July, after taking my GCSE in English, Maths, Physics, History, French and Art. I have represented the school in cricket and table tennis, and attend the debating society very regularly, having been the main speaker on several occasions. Outside school, I play for the Fenton junior cricket eleven and enjoy swimming; I have just obtained my gold life-saving certificate.

However, my main interest is photography. I helped to set up the school photographic society and I am its secretary this year. For the last two years I have been a member of the Fenton Camera Club; I contributed to the exhibition of the club's work which was displayed in the Fenton Public Library last winter and I attend all its meetings. On Saturdays and two evenings a week I work at Guildhall Cameras as a sales assistant; I am also entrusted with some of the repair work.

I am very keen to make my career in photography and the vacancy at your studios is just the sort of job I am looking for. You would find me eager and quick to learn, and very conscientious.

My headmaster, Mr. D. L. Leyton, and Mrs. S. Henshaw, manageress of Guildhall Cameras, 24, Cherrytree Lane, Fenton have both agreed to provide references if you need them.

I look forward to hearing from you soon and hope very much that I am asked to come to an interview.

Yours sincerely,

D Campbell

David Campbell

13 A curriculum vitae

DAVID PAUL CAMPBELL

Personal details

Address: 180 Fulford Road, Fenton, Surrey FN7 8YG.

Telephone: Fenton 83651

Date of birth: 4th January, 1970

Secondary education

Dates	School	GCE subjects to be taken June 1986
1981-	St Mark's Secondary School, Newcastle Street, Fenton.	English, Maths, Physics, History, French, Art.

School interests

Photographic Society: helped set up the society and am now secretary.

Senior Debating Society: regular attendance at fortnightly meetings.

Sport: captain of house table tennis team and member of school team; member of school 1st cricket XI 1985.

Interests outside school

Photography: member of Fenton Camera Club since 1984. Contributed to the club's exhibition of work at Fenton Public Library 1985.

Sport: Fenton Junior Cricket XI 1985 season. Swimming and life-saving.

Work experience

Dates	Employer	Duties
1984-5	F. Scott, Newsagent's	Morning deliveries.
1985-	Guildhall Cameras	Sales assistant and some repair work; Saturdays and two weekday evenings.

Other experience and qualifications

Activity holidays: North Wales 1984; Brittany 1985.

Gold life-saving certificate 1985.

Referees

1. Mr D.L. Leyton, Headmaster, St Mark's Secondary School, Newcastle Street, Fenton.

2. Mrs S. Henshaw, Manageress, Guildhall Cameras, 24, Cherrytree Lane, Fenton.

A letter to accompany a *curriculum vitae*

180 Fulford Road,
Fenton, FN7 8YG.

3rd April, 19-

Mr. R. Caulfield,
Image Studios,
6, The Precinct,
Fenton.

Dear Mr. Caulfield,

I would like to apply for the position of general assistant which was advertised in this week's 'Fenton Post'.

I am enclosing a copy of my curriculum vitae, and you will see how interested I am in photography. I get a great deal of enjoyment from my involvement with the school photographic society and Fenton Camera Club, and I have found my work at Guildhall Cameras has greatly increased my understanding of the technical side of the subject.

I am very keen to work in studios like yours and to make a career in photography. I am eager to learn and am sure you would be pleased with the way I approached and performed my work.

I hope to hear from you soon.

Yours sincerely,

D Campbell

David Campbell

14 A debate speech

The conclusion of a speech opposing blood sports:

Now we must consider for a moment the proposer's claim that animals are always given the chance to save themselves. A chance to save themselves? Perhaps he can tell us how much of a chance the bull has of surviving a bull-fight. Or how many badgers escape with their lives after being tied to a stake surrounded by a pack of dogs. Surely in these cases the death of the animal is a foregone conclusion? It is true, of course, that the fox may be lucky enough to escape being torn to pieces and the game bird may be only winged, not killed, by the shotgun pellets. But does this really make such sports any more acceptable? I'd have thought that if it is wrong to kill an animal for sport, then it is wrong to *try* to kill it, whether or not you succeed. It would be interesting to know what opinions the fox and the bird themselves have on the matter.

So we have now examined the proposer's three main arguments – his arguments that blood sports help control pests, that animals do not experience suffering the way we would in similar circumstances and that they are always given a chance to escape. We have certainly not found any of these arguments convincing. However, there is a final point I want to make. Even if everything he has said were true, I would still want to ask: What sort of human being gets pleasure from killing? What kind of person gets his fun from an activity whose sole purpose is to end a life? Surely it is a barbaric mind that enjoys inflicting pain and death, and neither you nor I nor any civilised man or woman wants to live in a society which condones barbarism. The proposer has said we would be interfering with his personal freedom if we stopped him killing and maiming innocent creatures. It's true, we would – just as we already interfere with the personal freedom of husbands who want to murder wives, parents who want to batter children and researchers who want to inflict unnecessary suffering on laboratory animals. And we have a right to interfere. We have a duty to interfere; because we have a duty to defend the standards of a civilised society and to defend the rights of creatures unable to speak for themselves.

I know I have spoken for the great majority of you in totally condemning these savage sports and the savage people who take part in them. When we vote on this motion we must make it resoundingly clear to these people that, as far as we are concerned, blood sports are a shameful offence against decency and compassion. They *must* be banned. Thank you.

15 A report making comparisons

Conclusions of a magazine report comparing personal stereos:

Verdict

It must be said immediately that if excellent sound quality is your main consideration, you are not likely to be content with any machine costing less than £140 – in which case I would suggest one of the Ultrasound models reviewed in our last issue.

Those of us with a less critical ear, however, should be well satisfied with the reproduction achieved by stereos in the £55–110 price-range. At the cheaper end of this range models will be found to be relatively heavy and bulky – about as genuinely portable as a car battery. For a machine that is really comfortable to carry for hours, we must look to the more expensive mini-stereos, and I consider the Datishi PS-83 (£92) to be the best available at the moment: it has auto-reverse, Dolby noise reduction and radio capability by means of a cassette insert. Moreover, since the PS-83 takes AA batteries, running costs are significantly lower than those of most of its competitors

Taika's K-014 (£105) is certainly an impressively engineered machine and is a little lighter and smaller than the Datishi; the remote control feature described above is also an attractive extra. It has no radio, however, and uses AAA batteries which are the same price as the Datishi's but last less than half the time: the Taika would, therefore, be considerably more expensive to run. The same is true of the Audiphone 25 (£100) and Schlegel's MS-8 (£90) and since they have no remote control and are generally less well finished than the Datishi and the Taika, there is little to recommend them.

The Johnston D7488 (£55) certainly deserves mention in view of its cheapness. It must be realised, however, that this is quite a heavy, large machine and much more basic than the models already discussed, though it does have FM radio. Although I found it awkward to use, sound quality was acceptable and it should be considered if your pocket will not stretch to what I believe to be the best buy: the Datishi PS-83.

16 A formal letter of complaint

39 St Stephen's Close,
Crenleigh.

12th July, 19-

Dear Mr Torrence,

I think you ought to know that David was very hurt by the remark you made yesterday when returning the History exam answers that you suspected him of having copied from the boy next to him. He is still terribly upset, as I am, by the accusation and the humiliation in front of his friends.

You must believe me when I say I know my son well enough to be sure he would never dream of cheating. Dishonesty of that sort just is not in his nature. I can only suggest if his answers were very similar to William Sutcliffe's, this may be explained by the fact that William and he did most of their revision for the exams together.

David has always enjoyed being taught by you and I do hope that you will be able to say something to him to make him see that you no longer suspect him of behaving wrongly.

Yours sincerely,

Mary Jamieson.

17 A formal letter making suggestions

11 Hereford Close,
Steadley.

4th April 19-

The Headmistress,
Thorncroft Green Secondary School,
Baldwin Road,
Steadley.

Dear Mrs. Goldsmith,

In the last newsletter you said that you would welcome parents' views concerning the proposal to raise the contributions pupils make to the school fund. It is suggested the contribution be increased from its present one pound a term to a single payment of five pounds to be made at the start of the school year. I am writing on behalf of several parents who have opinions on the matter.

First, we would like to raise a more general question concerning the school fund itself and the use to which it is put. In the newsletter you say that most of the money goes towards running and maintaining the school minibus and that, without the proposed increase, sports teams would need to pay for transport when they attend away fixtures. However, relatively few children are involved in this use of the minibus, and when it is used for other purposes - theatre trips, for example - pupils are charged for transport. Since there is obviously the danger that some parents might consider their children are not benefiting from the free transport the school fund is being used to provide, we feel it would be helpful if, in the next newsletter, you explained the school's policy on this matter.

Regarding the suggested increase, we wish to make three points:

1. With unemployment so high in this area, even raising the contributions by only two pounds could well cause some families difficulty.
2. We understand, of course, that a single payment in September would be simpler to collect, but many parents would find it easier to cope with three spaced instalments. We do think it would be better, therefore, to continue termly payments.
3. You do say: 'The school would treat cases of financial hardship sympathetically.' However, we feel that even parents who are very poorly off might be reluctant to plead poverty and possibly embarrass their children by doing so.

We know from past experience that you will consider our views seriously and understand that we have only the good of the school community at heart.

Yours sincerely,

Elizabeth Williamson.

Elizabeth Williamson

18 Newspaper articles reporting surveys

Increase in child smoking worries DHSS ministers

by Diane Spencer

A new survey showing that one in five secondary school pupils smokes has alarmed Government ministers.

The survey by the Office of Population Censuses and Surveys suggests that the number of child smokers is increasing in some age groups – particularly 14- and 15-year-old girls.

And the Government has reacted to the report by announcing it is to spend £1 million on a television campaign aimed at 11- to 16-year-olds.

Mr Rory Whitney, Parliamentary Under Secretary for Health, said that there was evidence that the great majority of adults who smoked took up the habit in their teenage years. "It is therefore vital that we step up our efforts to dissuade youngsters from starting to smoke in the first place."

The survey covered 9,234 pupils in almost 300 schools in Great Britain in 1984. A similar survey was carried out in 1982.

The new survey showed:

- a disturbing increase in the number of fourth-year girls taking up smoking: 24 per cent compared with 15 per cent in 1982, whereas the number of boys rose by 2 per cent;
- 22 per cent of all secondary school pupils smoked (19 per cent in 1982);
- 13 per cent smoked regularly, a 2 per cent increase on 1982; and
- 31 per cent of boys smoked regularly in the fifth year (1982: 26 per cent), while the figure for girls stayed at 28 per cent.

Judging by the survey, which was carried out for the Department of Health and Social Security, boys experiment with smoking earlier than girls, but girls catch up during their second year. It also suggests that almost a quarter of regular smokers have 10 or more cigarettes a day.

There was little regional variation in the sample. Welsh teenagers smoked slightly fewer cigarettes and the prevlence was higher in southern England than elsewhere in England and Wales.

Pupils who smoked were more likely to have parents and brothers and sisters who smoked. In England and Wales 29 per cent of pupils whose brothers and sisters smoked were regular smokers, compared with 8 per cent of pupils with non-smoking siblings.

Although most pupils accepted that smoking was associated with health risks, about one-third thought smoking was only harmful to those who smoked a lot.

The survey suggests that 11 to 15-year-olds are smoking between 19.6 and 26 million cigarettes a week – at an annual cost of between £70 million and £90 million.

Smoking among secondary school children in 1984, by Joy Dobbs and Alan Marsh, OPCS social survey division. HMSO £10.50.

THE TIMES EDUCATIONAL SUPPLEMENT
6 DECEMBER 1985

More leisure enjoyed at home

An Englishman's home is becoming an increasingly popular and expensive castle with an estimated £36 billion, or an average of £1,800 per family, now being spent annually on leisure pursuits in British homes.

Nearly two-thirds of British families prefer to spend their free time in the comfort of their own home, according to a Gallup survey published yesterday.

For most adults and older children watching television remains the dominant spare-time activity, but the survey concluded that families are viewing less and spending more time on other home-based activities.

Women prefer to read in their spare time, men spend more time reading newspapers and magazines, those aged 13 to 15 spend more time listening to records and tapes, those aged 6 to 12 spend more time riding bicycles and under fives prefer to play with toys.

The survey, commissioned by F. W. Woolworth, was based on interviews with 1,005 women with at least one child under 16.

Nearly half of the family households owned a video player and three out of ten families were found to settle down with a take-away meal and watch a video at least once a week.

The survey found men four times as likely as women to be responsible for fixing things around the house, and over a quarter of men and one fifth of women do some painting and decorating at least once a week.

TRENDS IN FAMILY LEISURE AT HOME – 1984/1985

Activities	% spending more or less time doing every week		
	more time	less time	% ch'nge
Watching TV	18	22	−4
Watching videos	14	8	+6
Listening to records and tapes	24	7	+17
Reading books	22	7	+15
Reading newspapers	13	6	+7
Giving parties	2	3	−1
Playing family games	20	4	+16
Working	16	3	+13

Regionally, women in the south were found to be less likely to carry out home repairs than those in the north and Scotland, while women in Wales are unlikely to do any at all.

Traditionally, family games such as snap and bridge are still more popular than computer games of the games families play together. Fifty-seven per cent of the families questioned play card or board games at least once a week.

THE TIMES
1 NOVEMBER 1985

19 Publicity for a cause

Bread not Bombs

The money required to provide adequate food, water, education, health and housing for everyone in the world has been estimated at $17 billion a year. It is a huge sum of money

...about as much as the world spends on arms every two weeks.

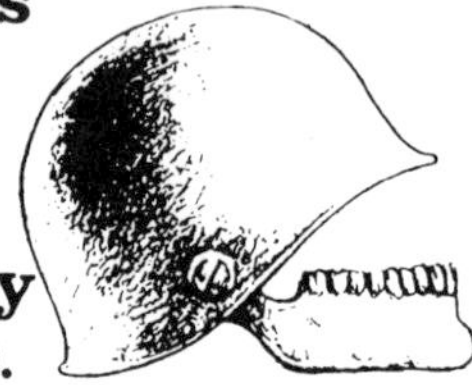

OXFAM

DID YOU KNOW ?

£6 of your money goes on arms every week. Next year it will be even more.

The amount the world spends on arms is going up all the time.

At the same time the small amount Britain gives in aid to poor countries is going down. 40,000 children die from hunger and disease every day.

Three quarters of the arms we export go to Third World countries. This takes away money desperately needed for food, shelter, health and education.

Even if these weapons are never used they are killing countless people.

SHOULDN'T WE SPEND MORE ON BREAD AND LESS ON BOMBS ?

Help us create a world that cares, not kills!

This outrage must be stopped.

Dogs and cats, much like the pet you may have, suffer horrifying cruelty in Asia. Anti-cruelty teams sent out by the International Fund for Animal Welfare (IFAW) have found terrified dogs bound with rope lying in dreadful pain in marketplaces waiting to be eaten by relatively well-off "gourmets"... dog meat is much more expensive than other staple food. The animals were muzzled with jagged tin cans and their front legs had been agonizingly dislocated by the manner in which they were tied. In one country we found dogs and cats being slowly strangled with cord before being butchered and eaten.

IFAW is determined to do all that can be done to end this torture. Public support has enabled us to provide a mobile veterinary clinic in one country where local vets now treat dogs and cats in desperate need. In Metro Manila we were instrumental in the passing of a law that actually prohibits the eating of cats and dogs.

A lot has been achieved but there is much, much more to do. We cannot continue this vital work, however, without your support. Your donation will help send IFAW anti-cruelty teams back to Asia where the animals desperately need our help.

IFAW

THE INTERNATIONAL FUND FOR ANIMAL WELFARE

I wish to be involved in your efforts to save the animals from cruelty in Asia.

Here is my contribution of £________

☐ Please tick if IFAW member. 5 ENKZ

Name________

Address________

____

________ Postcode________

Please post your donation to: International Fund for Animal Welfare, Section 133, Tubwell House, New Road, Crowborough, East Sussex, TN6 2QH.

20 Advertisements

Could you help point today's teenagers in the right direction?

Being an Officer or Instructor in the Army Cadet Force is a spare time activity that calls for some very special qualities.

You don't have to be an ex-Regular to do it well, nor must you have had any special training – we can provide that.

What *is* important, is that you should have a real interest in young people and take pleasure in helping them develop the kind of qualities that Cadet membership encourages. Such as self-reliance, initiative and integrity.

The Army Cadet Force provides an interest and focus for thousands of teenagers aged between 13-18 years, offering all kinds of outdoor activities, sports and skills such as map reading, fieldcraft and first aid.

If you're interested and aged between 19 and 40 you'll find there are few activities more rewarding than the ACF.

As an Officer or Instructor you'll have to be prepared to be away some weekends and spend up to two weeks a year at Summer Camp, for which time you'll be paid, of course.

But our Officers and Instructors find themselves quite happily putting in a couple of evenings each week, for the sheer satisfaction the job brings.

Proving that the real rewards of the job have more to do with the young people themselves than the pay you receive.

For further information contact your local County ACF HQ or TAVR Association (they're in the phone book under Army) or fill in the coupon and send it to: Capt. Andrew North, Cadet Training Centre, Frimley Park, Camberley, Surrey GU16 5HD.

Name __________

Address __________

__________ Age (19-40) __________

ARMY CADET FORCE

FOR FRIENDSHIP, LOVE OR MARRIAGE Dateline *is the way to meet*

- **LONGEST ESTABLISHED**
  In the last 20 YEARS Dateline has created many thousands of love stories, the result of over half a million Dateline introductions each year.
- **WHO JOINS DATELINE?**
  Everyone! People of all ages from all professions and trades, from every walk of life. People just like you! Most importantly, when you join Dateline YOU CHOOSE the sort of people you want to meet.
- **NATIONWIDE**
  Dateline members come from all over the country, and the number of members in each area is constantly being renewed and added to by local and national advertising.
- **INEXPENSIVE**
  Dateline is certainly the best VALUE FOR MONEY service, simply providing more people for you to meet.
- **RESPONSIBLE**
  20 years of experience, and a caring approach, give us a justifiable pride in the professional, reliable and confidential service we provide.
- **MORE PEOPLE TO MEET**
  Dateline is the LARGEST computer dating agency in the world; and the more Dateline members there are, the more people we have for you to meet. However, size has not made us impersonal. We are not just a box number; our friendly staff are always happy to help you either in our London office or on the telephone.
- **WE CARE**
  We want your membership of Dateline to be successful, whether it's friendship, love or marriage you are seeking, so our Dateline system and personal service are geared to cater for your individual requirements.
- **PROVEN SUCCESS**

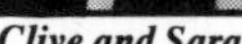

Clive and Sara
To Clive, after his divorce, joining Dateline seemed 'logical', and to Sara, a single parent, it was simply a decision to 'do something' about her social life. Attraction grew to love, and six months later they were married.

Suzanne and Tim
'I thought Suzanne was too attractive to be a member of Dateline. I thought the only people who used dating agencies were the real lonely hearts types, but not at all!' Suzanne and Tim are now married.

**** you meet such nice people through Dateline***

Dateline is a member of the Association of British Introduction Agencies 29 Manchester St. London W1.

For free details about Dateline and how it works in successfully matching people like you, send this coupon today to: Dateline, 23 Abingdon Rd., London W8 6AH. Tel: 01.938 1011

Dateline

Name ....

Age .... Sex ....

Address ....

....

....

Postcode ....

RDA

WITH FOUR WHEEL DRIVE, THE GRANADA 4x4 HAS PHENOMENAL TRACTION. BUT WITH ABS BRAKES IT'S GOT STOPPING POWER TO MATCH.

Here's something to think about before you buy a car with four wheel drive. You'll find you've got more traction on wet or greasy roads than ever before. You'll have more grip in corners. And if it snows this winter you'll leave everyone else standing. Or struggling to fit snow chains.

But don't forget, when a car is able to go well in such treacherous conditions it's doubly important that it can stop well. Which brings us to the new two mile a minute plus,† fuel injected, 2.8 Granada 4x4.

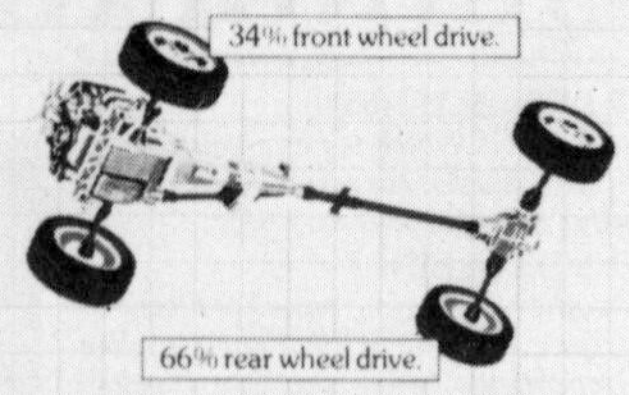

In the Granada 4x4 the drive is biased towards the rear wheels to give you predictable handling characteristics. It grips without vices.

Not only does it have the most advanced four wheel drive system in production. But it also has ABS brakes fitted as standard equipment.

In case you're not familiar with the ABS system this is how it works. Imagine it's raining. You're forced to brake hard and swerve round an obstacle, a tractor for instance.

With ordinary brakes it would be very easy to lock the wheels and skid straight on. ABS is designed to stop that happening. The system can sense when a wheel starts to lock and release the brake on that wheel for a fraction of a second till adhesion is regained. That way you can stop far quicker than you could with your wheels locked.

ABS brakes: If the system 'feels' a wheel begin to lock it can release and re-apply the brakes 15 times a second until adhesion is regained.

And steer safely.

This combination of four wheel drive and ABS makes the Granada 4x4 the most sure footed luxury express you could possibly imagine.

Take a test drive soon and see why 'Motor' said "Perhaps one day all cars will be like this."

Ford

Granada Ghia 4x4 illus. at £15,464.
Maximum retail price excluding number plates and delivery.
Also available is the Granada Scorpio 4x4. †Ford computed figures.

Index of language types

Page numbers in bold type refer to items in the Resource File.

Advertising
promotion of products etc 58 **116–8**
publicity for causes and points of view 77 **114–5**
Advice leaflets 5 **93–4**
Articles
advice in magazines and newspapers 33 **101**
news articles 48 **103**
reviews and reports in school magazines 41
surveys reported in newspapers and magazines 87 **112–3**
Descriptions of machines 9 **95**
Directions 15 **97**
Instructions 12 **96**
Formal letters
arrangements 37 **102**
complaints 68 **110**
job applications and curricula vitae 54 **105–7**
to newspapers 81
reports on situations 52 **104**
suggestions 73 **111**
Personal letters – persuasion 44
Minutes of meetings 85
Reports
comparisons 64 **109**
eyewitness statements 22
factual accounts for forms 2 **92**
personal reports 18 **98**
situations reported in letters 52 **104**
Speech
debate speeches 62 **94** **108**
discussion 85
prepared talks intended to persuade 26
radio commentary 30 **99–100**

Acknowledgements

The author is most grateful to Mr Roy Blatchford, Miss Karen Clark, Mrs E M Dyche, Miss Samantha Farlie, Miss Amanda Smithard, Miss Trudy Staples and Mr M R Turner for their advice and practical help in the preparation of this book.

We are grateful to the following for permission to include copyright material:

Associated Book Publishers (UK) Ltd for an abridged extract from pp 152–158 *The Secret Diary of Adrian Mole Aged 13¾* by S Townsend (Methuen London); the author, R Balchin for an extract from *Emergency Aid in Schools* (pub by the Order of St John Ambulance); the author, M Baldwin for an abridged extract from pp 148–157 *Grandad with Snails* (Unicorn Books 1962); The British Broadcasting Corporation for extracts from pp 160–161, 203, 325–326 *War Report: D Day to VE Day* compiled and edited by D Hawkins; the author's agents for 'The Song of the Battery Hen' by E Brock from *Penguin Modern Poets*; the Controller of Her Majesty's Stationery Office for data and abridged tables from *Young People in the 80s Survey* (Dept of Science 1983) Crown Copyright; the Institute for the Study of Drug Dependence for an adapted extract from p 23 *Drug Abuse Briefing* by M Ashton Copyright ISDD 1985; the Executors of the Estate of K S P McDowall and William Heinemann Ltd for extracts from pp 236–239 *Mapp and Lucia* by E F Benson; the National Farmers' Union for a rewritten version of the pamphlet 'The Case for Cages' (orig pub 1979); The New Yorker Magazine Inc for the short story 'The Test' by Angelica Gibbs from *The New Yorker* (15/6/60) © 1940, 1968 The New Yorker Magazine Inc; Sinclair Vehicle Sales Ltd for specifications of the Sinclair C5; Times Newspapers Ltd for the articles 'Increase in child smoking worries DHSS ministers' by Diane Spencer from *The Times Educational Supplement* (6/12/85) and 'Loophole Wagon' from *The Times* (11/1/85); TV Times for extracts from the 'Dear Katie' column in *TV Times* (3–9/11/84) © 1986 ITP Ltd.

We are grateful to the following for permission to reproduce photographs and other copyright material:

Associated Press, page 23; Stuart Banks, *The Complete Handbook of Poultry-Keeping*, Ward Locke, page 77; Council of Territorial, Auxiliary and Volunteer Reserve Associations, page 116; Dateline International, page 117; Department of the Environment, *The Heavy Cost of Motoring*, reproduced by permission of the Controller of Her Majesty's Stationery Office, page 93; Ford Motor Company, page 118; International Fund for Animal Welfare, page 115; Oxfam, page 114; PGL Young Adventure, pages 44, 45 and 46; W Heath Robinson, drawing from *Railway Ribaldry*, Laurence Pollinger, page 52; Ann Ronan Picture Library, pages 9 and 10; Sealink British Ferries, page 37 and 38; Sinclair Vehicles, page 61; *South Eastern Newspapers*, page 103; *The Times*, page 113; *Times Educational Supplement*, page 112.